Affirmations for Black Men

Life-Changing Affirmations for Success, Confidence, Health & Wealth That Will Drastically Boost Your Mindset and Increase Your Happiness

Willie Brown

©Copyright 2021 – Willi Brown - All rights reserved

The content within this book may not be reproduced, duplicated, or transmitted without direct written permission from the author or the publisher.

Under no circumstances will any blame or legal responsibility be held against the publisher, or author, for any damages, reparation, or monetary loss due to the information contained within this book, either directly or indirectly.

Legal Notice

This book is copyright protected. This book is only for personal use. You cannot amend, distribute, sell, use, quote, or paraphrase any part, or the content within this book, without the consent of the author-publisher.

Disclaimer Notice

Please note that the information contained within this document is for educational and entertainment purposes only. All effort has been executed to present accurate, up-to-date, and reliable, complete information. No warranties of any kind are declared or implied. Readers acknowledge that the author is not engaging in the rendering of legal, financial, medical, or professional advice.

Table of Contents

Introduction 5

Chapter 1 Positive Affirmations 7

Chapter 2 The Power of Affirmations 15

Chapter 3 Daily Affirmations for Positive Thoughts 19

Chapter 4 We Are All Humans and no Human is Inferior 26

Chapter 5 Why You Should Love Yourself 29

Chapter 6 How to Eliminate the Feeling of "Not Good Enough" 33

Chapter 7 Take Responsibility for Your Life 36

Chapter 8 The Instigator of Confidence 39

Chapter 9 We all Need Good Counselors 42

Chapter 10 The True Test of the Value of Your Desire 45

Chapter 11 Use It to Your Advantage 47

Chapter 12 You Deserve It 50

Chapter 13 The Choice is Yours to Make 52

Chapter 14 Affirmations for Self-Esteem 54

Chapter 15 Affirmations for Self-Love 69

Chapter 16 Affirmations for Accepting Yourself 94

Chapter 17 Affirmations for Controlling Yourself and Your Surroundings 106

Chapter 18 Affirmations for Relationships and Supporting Others 122

Chapter 19 Affirmations for Taking Accountability and Responsibility 134

Chapter 20 Affirmations for Self-Confidence 147

Chapter 21 Affirmations for Increasing Productivity and Improving Decision Making 170

Chapter 22 Affirmations for Success 186

Chapter 23 Affirmations for Building, Keeping, and Growing Wealth . 203

Chapter 24 Affirmations for Attitude and Relationship with Money 231

Chapter 25 Affirmations for Handling Professional, Work, and Business Stress 248

Chapter 26 Affirmations for Protecting and Improving Your Mental State and Confidence 258

Chapter 27 Affirmations for Gratitude 270

Chapter 28 Financial Affirmations for Every Day 283

Chapter 29 Breaking Bad Habits 314

Chapter 30 Building Constructive Habits 321

Chapter 31 On Sadness 329

Chapter 32 On Happiness 336

Chapter 33 Setting Short-Term Goals 343

Chapter 34 Setting Long-Term Goals 351

Conclusion 358

Introduction

We both know that being a fearless, successful man in this competitive world and doing it while black is one of the hardest things in life. You will always be judged and cast off as if you are not equal to what society says. You are continuously belittled as if your thoughts and ideas aren't good enough.

You are ridiculed, criticized, and laughed at behind your back because you are simply never the best or as good as you know you are. The world may not say this, but it's how we feel deep inside. I've been there. My question is, how can we get through our days as if it does not bother us? As if it has no impact on the true potential we have inside us. It feels as though we don't have an answer. I am here to tell you, we do.

You are meant to shine bright, brother, in this world as if your spark of light is the centerpiece to your purpose. Because it is. Today is when you let go of all the insecurities, fears, and inhibitions that have held onto you for dear life and let the masterful power of your true inner man guide your way. Remember that you are a successful black man; you are smart, you are likeable, you are compatible, and you are a good looking person that any reasonable woman would want to be with.

You will never want for anything. You will never be jealous of anyone who has more than you because you already have more than you even know. I will teach you how to use your mind and heart to amplify every fiber of your soul.

Remember that you are a black man. Wealth and prosperity are bestowed upon your inner self. I call this affirmation because it's a reminder of who you are, and who you can be. It reminds you that all you are and meant to be creates your future. You are the limitless version of yourself. You are a black man surrounded by hate from those who will never understand you. Anger and hatred are not your attributes. As a black man, turn your back on hate.

You will not turn your back on love because love is your greatest strength; it's in your heart and in your soul. Learn to appreciate life, brother. Embrace love. Be a loving, kind, and patient person. Be what the world needs from you. Hold those feelings of anger and hate very close to your heart and squeeze it tight, until it's no longer a problem. Unlock the gate inside you to the empowering power you were designed to be.

Stop looking outside yourself to find who you are; you're going to be put yourself under intense pressure should you attempt it. You can never see your true self from the perspective of someone else - only through your own inner vision.

Look within. You're the only one who can define you. the perception you have of yourself comes from within you to make you feel loved and valuable and spur you to aspire to become the best you can be in life.

You're the only one who holds the key to the lock that contains your happiness and self-satisfaction. You can only find that key by looking inside yourself rather than around you. As you look within and at yourself after going through this book, you will see a different, positive and new version of you. You'll see the need to lavish love on yourself daily because you know you greatly deserve it.

Chapter 1
Positive Affirmations

Law of Attraction and the Power of Your Belief

You've definitely heard of the notion of a half-full or half-empty glass and how simple it is to identify someone who is optimistic or pessimistic when they use that concept to their advantage. Take note, however, that whether the individual is an optimist or a pessimist, he or she is successfully altering reality depending upon his or her temperament. Essentially, this implies that the optimist will only see water while the pessimist only sees nothingness, yet they are both true in a certain way.

The law of attraction operates in a similar manner: your thoughts have the ability to distort reality, and if you have a pessimistic outlook on life, you are more likely to draw terrible occurrences into your world. Take note of how many negative people are trapped in a cycle where they are unable to maintain a positive disposition any longer as a result of the numerous negative events that continue to occur in their lives. But the reason for the numerous negative events continuing to occur in their lives is that they are unable to maintain a positive disposition.

The law of attraction is based on the concept of "polarity," which is the idea that everything in the universe contains either a positive or a negative kind of energy. It states that everything, from the food you eat to the people you talk to, to the things you say, to the things you think contains either a positive or a negative energy, depending upon your perspective. It's important to note that being around individuals who moan or yell a lot may make you feel lousy even if you're not directly experiencing what they're going through — this is the law of attraction at work.

When you put your attention on the bad, more negative events will occur in your life. When you put your attention on the good, on the other hand, more of the same will come your way in the future.

Fortunately, there is a method to influence the law of attraction and make it work in your favor: altering your thoughts via the use of positive affirmation and the power of manifestation. Positive affirmations provide you with a new set of eyes through which to see the world, and as a result, they give you the confidence to do many things you never imagined were possible.

How to Use Affirmation Effectively

Believe it or not, some affirmations may cause more harm than good. For example, have you ever told a friend not to be nervous and ended up making him twice as nervous as he already was? The mind is clever, and it won't give up its disposition without a fight, so here's what we do to make effective affirmations:

- **Turn declarative affirmations into interrogative affirmations** – One of the most recent findings in behavioral psychology is that people are more willing to admit defeat in an argument if asked questions instead of being attacked by argumentative statements. For example, if you're nervous about giving a company presentation, you tell yourself, "I'm going to do great! I've practiced all night and I've done this man times before," Instead, ask yourself, "Last time I've presented, people were amazed at how entertaining and informative my slides were. What can I do to make this presentation even better?" By giving yourself concrete questions to answer, the brain doesn't think it needs to defend itself. Use this tip whenever positive declarative affirmations don't seem to work.

- **Be specific with your affirmations** – In order for your brain and the Universe to collaborate properly, you have to be clear about what you want. A lot of people have problems identifying exactly what they want but have no trouble identifying what they hate. If you're one of those people who notice the negatives more than the positives, don't fret; a simple workaround is to find the opposite of the things that you hate. For example, find a song you really hate to the point that you cringe and squirm whenever it plays on the radio. Now find what you believe is the opposite of that song in terms of how it makes you feel. In most cases, the opposite is your favorite song. In short, if you know something that makes you unhappy, then chances are, the opposite of that will make you happy.

Here are step-by-step instructions on probing areas of your life that need positive affirmations:

1. Write down your regular daily routine

2. Separate the things you experience into three columns:

   A. Events you enjoy experiencing

   B. Events you don't enjoy experiencing

   C. Events that don't really evoke a strong emotional response.

3. For column B, look for the complete opposite of that event and list it in column A. For example, if column B contains a statement like "never getting a good night's sleep and always waking up groggy and tired," it should be converted to something like "having a restful sleep and waking up feeling refreshed, alert, and ready to face the day!" and placed in column A.

4. For column C, look for the positive version of that event and list it in column A. For example, if column C contains a statement like "eating breakfast," it could be converted to something like

"eating a healthy, delicious breakfast that'll keep me energized throughout the day" and placed in column A.

5. Column A should now contain specific events in your life that you can use as a starting point for positive affirmations!

- **Be consistent with your affirmations** – a phenomenon has been observed where people who use their goals and dreams as passwords to accounts they access everyday end up achieving those goals and dreams. This has everything to do with the fact that people are compelled to write these objectives and desires again and over again, causing them to soak into the darkest recesses of their subconscious minds. By consistently affirming yourself at least thrice a day, your mind will eventually learn to accept a better form of a reality you've crafted.

- **Believe your affirmations** – Telling yourself that you are calm and relaxed before an interview doesn't mean you're going to deny that you're nervous. On the contrary, you're actually acknowledging your nervousness and then positively affirming to overcome it. If you notice that you're reacting in a very strong and negative manner when you try to affirm yourself, try to apply the tip regarding converting declarative affirmations into interrogative affirmations. It's extremely important to believe what you're telling yourself; otherwise you'll be subconsciously affirming the opposite.

- **Imagine your affirmations** – Humans are visual creatures, which means we absorb information better when in a form that we can visualize. If you're affirming the financial aspect of your life, imagine performing the required steps in achieving that goal. Imagine waking up early, talking to more clients, doing some additional studying, etc. Then imagine reaching that goal and how your life will be changed by your actions and sacrifices. This should be repeated many times until you no longer feel disconnected from the scenario you're in. Do this until it feels too real to let go.

Benefits of Positive Affirmation

Positive affirmation isn't just the act of trying to "fake it 'til you make it." Rather, positive affirmation is the act of focusing on positive values, making you more resilient to stress and other gunk you don't need in your life. If that alone doesn't convince you, here are some more benefits of positive affirmation:

- Positive affirmation lets you see the water in the half-filled glass. Going back to the analogy of the pessimist and the optimist, the optimist will be able to water a wilting plant, quench someone's thirst, clean something, etc. with the water he sees. The pessimist, on the other hand, sees nothing but a lack of water to fill the cup and does nothing until the remaining amount of water completely evaporates. Using the power of affirmation you open up worlds of possibilities you never thought existed, which will definitely give you more opportunities to do the things that make you happy.

- Positive affirmation gives you control. By practicing positive affirmation, you will have much better control over different aspects of your life simply because you're more aware of the events that hurt you and those that help you. In fact, you are consciously making an effort to choose the latter.

- Positive affirmation doesn't have to be a mundane ritual; positive affirmation isn't just to help you make great company presentations or helping you overcome stress. Positive affirmation is also to help you achieve new goals and dreams! You can positively affirm yourself with a power chant or even a power stance to enforce your ideas. In a sense, positive affirmation is already a positive event in your daily routine!

The Power of Repeated Words and Thoughts

REMEMBER how you would repeatedly say a phrase or a sentence in order to remember it for a test? In most cases, repeated words and ideas have the tendency to become permanent when done over a period of time. By repeating your affirmations over and over again, your subconscious will gradually accept and believe what you're saying to yourself.

Reprogramming the Subconscious Mind

The subconscious mind is the most powerful portion of the brain, but it's also the hardest to manage since it's always changing. Everything you really want in life is stored in your subconscious mind, including your aspirations, goals, anxieties, and nightmares.

Because the subconscious mind has not been persuaded, certain affirmations will not function because the subconscious will continue to attract bad experiences. In order for your affirmations to begin to have an impact on your life, you must first fool your subconscious mind into embracing your affirmations.

Here are some tips to help your affirmations get through to your subconscious mind:

- **Find the balance between ambitious and realistic** – a lot of people go overboard with their affirmations. Some people who are earning very little and are buried in debt might say, "I am rich and I earn $100,000 per month." Of course, the subconscious mind knows right away that this isn't true. One way to fix this is not necessarily to tone down the dream, but to add more realism into it, e.g., "I have the strength and determination to free myself from debts and work harder to earn $100,000 per month."

- **Give your subconscious mind proof that your affirmations are true** – affirmation alone won't change your life; you have to mix in action as well. Affirmations like "I have a muscular physique" are useless if not combined with proper exercise, rest, and nutrition. A better version of the previous affirmation would be, "I choose to work out at least three times for a week, get at least seven hours of sleep, and eat healthy meals in order to keep my strong physique."

- **Create affirmations that evoke strong emotions** – notice how a lot of people remember quite easily events that made them cry, laugh, etc. Make sure that when you create affirmations, you include adjectives that evoke happy, inspiring, and motivational thoughts. Instead of saying, "I choose to wake up early every morning," say, "I choose to wake up early every morning feeling recharged, refreshed, and ready to take on the day!"

- **Make sure your affirmation targets you** – tailor your affirmations especially for yourself. For example, an affirmation like "my boss will give me a promotion" is rather weak because that affirmation targets your boss and not you, i.e., you do not have any control over your boss. Instead, opt for something like "I choose to feel that I always get quality work turned in and therefore deserve a promotion."

Using Positive Affirmations to Change Your Life

The human brain hates change; it tries its best to remain in a state where it spends minimal energy, which translates to being lazy and unsuccessful. Positive affirmations trick the brain into thinking that you're already living the life you want, and therefore it more readily accepts the necessary changes that have to happen in your life.

What would you actually do if you happen to wake from a very long sleep and were told that you are an astronaut, a soldier, or a doctor, etc.? You'd probably act differently. You'd talk more confidently, you'd walk more confidently, and basically, you'd be a completely different person. You'd easily surpass your previously self-imposed limits because you believe that you've already overcome them. Like the half-filled glass, you now see your body's capabilities instead of its limitations. By leveraging the power of positive affirmations, you'll be able to tap into your subconscious mind and reprogram it to give you the life you've always wanted.

Chapter 2
The Power of Affirmations

Affirmations have real self-motivating power. You may or may not be good to yourself or accept yourself. You may be confident or, on the other hand, not sure of yourself. You may be positive or negative, happy or unhappy, depending upon what you say to yourself.

Whenever a situation causes nervousness or worry, declaring these statements will help you overcome the difficulties and initiate the changes you want to see in your body. For these changes to be positive and lasting, you must treat yourself with love and kindness, that is to say, as you would treat a friend.

When you start losing weight, whether for health or aesthetic reasons, it is not always easy to stay the course in the long term. Thanks to positive affirmations, you will be able to gain motivation and self-esteem to continue on.

What are Positive Affirmations?

To make positive affirmations is to speak positive words to yourself out loud (preferably when alone!). There is a personal development technique used to retrain your brain to think more optimistically. You may make positive comments regarding your health, your job, or even your self-confidence, relationships, and other aspects of your life.

The goal is to attract happiness by pronouncing it! At first, one does not believe frankly in what one says. The lyrics are even the opposite of what we think but by dint of saying it, the brain will believe it, and so will we! This is how they will have a real impact on our lives.

Examples of statements to lose weight

- I take care of myself and it makes me feel good
- I feel better and better
- I am proud not to give in to gluttony, bad for my health
- Each day brings me a little closer to my goal
- I have a healthy life and I eliminate my bad habits
- I lose weight because I love myself (not because I don't like my body)
- I can do it

How to Create a Powerful Positive Affirmation?

The start of a new year allows us to take stock and set inspiring goals. Have you thought about what you want to do, get, achieve and become in 2022? We suggest you create powerful positive affirmations for each of your goals.

Experience the Magic of Performance

Affirmations will help you identify those aspects that are most important to you. You can test your goals with the "12 questions from the coach." This will ensure that each goal is inspiring and truly beneficial for you. These questions will help you, for example, to identify the internal conflicts that can sometimes block the achievement of your goals. Here are some guidelines before you start creating a positive affirmation. Make sure your goal isn't causing you unwanted los.

Avoid the goals that force you to say, for example, "But if I do that, I won't have time to see my friends anymore."

The affirmation grows stronger each time it is repeated. You have to repeat it out loud with as much emotion as you possible can. The best times to repeat your affirmation are in the morning (waking up) and before going to bed.

We are now ready to begin. Complete the following table for each of your goals, following the guidelines. State the objective clearly and precisely.

Example: I would not like to be overweight

Your objective: put the statement in the first person singular.

Example: I do not want excess weight

Your objective: The affirmation must be positive.

You have to say what you want rather than what you don't want.

Example: I want to lose weight

Your objective: Add adjectives and superlatives

Example: I want to be super slim, have a healthy, athletic, and balanced body.

Your objective: Add numbers and details.

You have to say when, how much, why, etc.

Example: I want to lose 10 kg before the end of February, be super slim, have a healthy, athletic, and balanced body

Your objective: Associate a gesture with the affirmation. The gesture must give strength and motivation.

Example: Clenching your fist with a smile.

Your objective: Add "or even better" at the end of the statement.

Example: I want to lose 10 kg before the end of February, be super slim, have a healthy, athletic, and balanced body, or even better.

Your objective: Repeat your affirmation twice a day. The greater the amount of emotion you put into it, the more powerful it is going to be.

Get into the game. Put enthusiasm and determination into it.

Chapter 3
Daily Affirmations for Positive Thoughts

There's actually nothing quite like the sound of a supercharger on a fast automobile or motorbike to get your heart racing. Wouldn't it be so great if you could turn your life into a supercharged machine? You can do it: it all begins with positive affirmations.

When it comes to how you go from one day to the next, affirmations are critical to your success. Even on your toughest days, positive affirmations serve as a gentle reminder to keep going. More significantly, they serve as a gentle reminder that you are deserving of good things in your life, despite of your past sins.

The Affirmations

1. I am a positive person.

2. I like to view things from the bright side.

3. Whenever something happens to me, I pause, reflect on the situation and then react.

4. My life is filled with joy.

5. I am constantly having positive thoughts.

6. I am feeling happy and strong.

7. This day is a fantastic day.

8. I am always super excited to wake up each day and have a productive day.

9. My heart is filled with love, joy and positivity.

10. I feel secure and confident.

11. I am good enough.

12. I reject all negative thoughts and I accept everything positive.

13. I live an interesting life full of adventure and excitement.

14. I am a happy person.

15. I attract positive people into my life.

16. When people think of the most joyful person in their life, they think of me.

17. I spread joy and happiness to everyone.

18. I am feeling lucky and grateful every day for everything I have.

19. Today is going to be a spectacular today.

20. My life is fantastic.

21. I attract pleasant and joyful people into my life.

22. I feel enthusiastic about everything that I pursue.

23. My days are filled with fun activities and laughter.

24. I can self-motivate instantly whenever I need to.

25. Every breath that I take, I breath in happiness.

26. I am in total control of my life and any negative thought that enters my mind, I immediately let it go and move on.

27. I use positive affirmations daily to become a happier person.

28. I'm constantly energized and full of life, which is a great feeling.

29. I am blessed with all the energy I have.

30. I have complete control over all of my emotions, and I am choosing to feel positive and pleasure right now.

31. I take on life with a calm and relaxed attitude.

32. I have deep relationships and feel connected to my close friends and family.

33. I spread love to people and receive even more love back.

34. My life is free of clutter, noise and drama.

35. The possibilities of life are endless and I make sure to make the most of every possibility.

36. I truly believe in myself.

37. I am making a permanent change to become a positive individual.

38. I am brave, strong and confident.

39. Every time that I fall, I get up with ease and try again.

40. I am dedicated and driven to achieve the goals that I have set for myself.

41. I see myself as a very happy person.

42. I am feeling optimistic about life.

43. I let go of things that I cannot control and focus on things that I have control over.

44. I trust myself in making good decisions.

45. My positivity comes within and is not affected by the outside world.

46. I am adding something special to this world.

47. I take every failure as a learning lesson because I know that I will eventually succeed.

48. Having a positive attitude has helped me be a happier person.

49. Other people enjoy being around me because they get to partake in my happiness.

50. I am always feeling amazing and I am grateful for it.

51. Every single day of my existence is filled with anticipation.

52. I attract positive people into my life.

53. I have all that I need and I am deeply grateful for everything I have.

54. I feel fulfilled and satisfied with my life.

55. I take on challenges and grow as a person every day.

56. I always achieve the goals that I set for myself.

57. I always tend to look for the positive aspects of any circumstance.

58. I am always feeling very happy.

59. I fully approve of the person I am.

60. I am loved and appreciated by other people.

61. Every new person I meet has good things to say about me.

62. I am feeling joyful every moment of life.

63. I deserve to live an amazing life.

64. The universe is helping my achieve my dreams.

65. I believe in my talents and skills, and I can achieve any goal I set for myself.

66. My life is a whirlwind of love and pleasure.

67. I am constantly filled with positive energy.

68. I feel inspired and motivated every day.

69. I become more and more positive every day that goes on.

70. I love myself and I love the life I'm living.

71. I receive love and kindness from my friends, family and even strangers.

72. I am living life to the fullest.

73. I always looking for the good in people.

74. I feel a sense of peace at all times.

75. My positive energy is a blessing to the people around me.

76. I feel safe, confident and enthusiastic about life.

77. I am experiencing joy and happiness every day.

78. I deserve love and respect.

79. I help other people become positive by being positive myself.

80. I always feel a surge of happiness at the start of every day.

81. The world is a better and more joyful place with me in it.

82. I have the power to let go of negativity and fill myself with positivity.

83. I feel alive and fresh.

84. Every time that I take a breath in, I feel myself being filled with peaceful energy.

85. I am a masterpiece.

86. I am worthy of feeling happy and being loved.

87. My life is absolutely wonderful and I look forward to each day.

88. I spread positivity at all times.

89. I am eternally thankful for the extraordinary life that I have been blessed with.

90. I am capable of accomplishing everything that I set my mind to.

91. I allow myself to feel happy.

92. I always carry a feeling of inner peace.

93. I am a relaxed person that people enjoy hanging out with.

94. My accomplishments gives a deep feeling of satisfaction.

95. I am living the best life that I can live.

96. Every minute of my incredible existence is one I cherish.

Chapter 4
We Are All Humans and no Human is Inferior

"Nobody can make you feel inferior if you don't think you're inferior."

Affirmation: I am not inferior to anyone.

Listen good: you are not inferior to anyone. Neither is your race inferior to any other race. When God created man, he created just one man and woman, and we all are descendants of that one man and woman. So we are all created equal, and we are all equal.

Race is a distinction created by man for political purposes. They do this to exploit, subjugate, and oppress those with different physical features than their kind. They came up with lots of negative concepts to justify their oppressive tendencies.

Do you know why blacks were singled out for oppression? It was because blacks were discovered to be very tough, strong, skillful, productive, and not easily infected by diseases or broken down. they can quickly adapt to any weather condition. Hence, the oppressors became intimidated by our wonderful traits; and since they have governmental power, the use it to subjugate and oppress us and try to limit us so we wouldn't manifest our true potentials and greatness.

They are intimidated by our toughness, strengths, and abilities. Do you know that we are responsible for the development of the US, the UK, and some of the world's developed nations? Yes, that is a fact! Go and read your history books and discover the truth of your greatness. Our skills and resources were exploited all in the guise of colonialism and slavery.

We built nations because we were skillful, strong, and challenged, and not because we were inferior. Can a qualified person be inferior? Can a tough and strong person be regarded as inferior? Read between the lines. They intended to break us down with their oppression and negative tags, yet we are still standing strong, pushing harder to show them that we cannot be broken.

They may use the law and armed forces to weigh us down, just as they have always done systematically, but we are still pushing harder, trying to let them know that they can never stop us from taking our rightful place.

They are intimidated by us. They are leery of our toughness, scared of our strength, and of what we can achieve should we be given the chance to express ourselves freely without any interference - like every other race. That is their fear and why they are trying all they can to break us and stop us from manifesting our true potential with their unjustifiable hate and oppression.

We always have to keep our heads up and keep moving forward. If they want to break you, please do not allow them to do so. Do not allow them to stop you from dreaming; do not allow them to stop you from reaching to higher heights; and do not allow them to stop you from believing in yourself and working hard to achieve the future you desire.

They have tried all they could, but we are still standing strong. Look at how far we've come. Look at what we have achieved despite the subjugation and oppression. Look at the changes we are making. Our voices are beginning to get heard, and we are on the verge of enthronement. Let's keep our heads up and aim for our goals. The more we climb higher, the more we scare the shit out of them, and the less their grip will be on us.

You are not inferior; you cannot be inferior, and you should never act inferior. God never created any race, and God only created humans – that is, the human race. Don't ever allow any man to judge, discriminate against or oppress you because of the color of your skin. That you are black is who you are, and neither you nor anybody else has the power to alter that.

You're great! You're created for a purpose: you're created to be great and created black. Embrace yourself and be proud of your blackness because you're created complete and excellent, and no one is superior to you.

Declare these words aloud to yourself:

- I am created by God
- I am created for a purpose
- I am created to be awesome
- I am created to be great
- And I am created black
- I am not inferior to anyone

Chapter 5
Why You Should Love Yourself

"The Only Gift You Owe Yourself Daily is Love."

Affirmation: I love everything about myself.

The number one thing you owe yourself each day is acceptance and love. Acceptance is being at peace with who you are, while love is making the most of who you are, that is, giving yourself the best treatment possible and a shot at life. You can't love anything you don't first accept.

I have come across people who never liked themselves, and you can see such self-hate in how they live their lives and their relationships with the people around them. They neither think anything good about themselves nor says anything nice because they see nothing good in themselves.

This is a difficult way to live as such a life has a constant companion sadness, anger, self-hate, worries, anxieties, insecurities, and a continuous feeling of worthlessness. No wonder such people can consciously engage in self-destructive acts and see nothing wrong in them.

If you dig deep into such people's lives to find out why they feel such way about themselves and always look down on themselves, you will discover that such people have great difficulty accepting themselves for who they are; hence, the problem they're having with treating themselves right.

You see them going about seeking validation and putting themselves at the mercy of others to be exploited and mistreated. They don't understand that they are the ones reflecting how others would treat or relate to them.

Let me tell you this: no one can treat or love you better than you treat or love yourself. And you will have great difficulty treating yourself right or loving yourself unless you first accept yourself.

No one will accept you if you don't first accept yourself. People might pretend to accept you, but their main aim for such acceptance is because they want to use or exploit you. True blessing can only come from within. That is the beginning of your accurate self-awareness, discovery, expression, manifestation, and love.

If you're someone who's always struggling to get validation or acceptance from others, then I must tell you that you're putting yourself in a disadvantaged position, and you can never get what you're looking for. One of the ways you identify a man who hasn't yet accepted himself for who he is and giving himself a daily dosage of self-love medication is how he treats and carries himself.

The way you hold yourself and go about your everyday life will be influenced by how highly or poorly you regard yourself and how accepting and loving you are of others. Some people are not nice to themselves, and they fail to carry themselves with pride. Such an attitude is usually due to a lack of self-acceptance and self-love.

You see them trying to please everyone to get validation, but they are always left drained, exploited, and feeling worse about themselves than they were before they embarked on their validation quest.

Let me repeat this again for emphasis' sake: No one can give you what you haven't first given to yourself. Also, no one can treat you better than you're already treating yourself. You can't claim to deserve acceptance, love, respect, and good treatment from others if you're not flooding your life with such goodness.

You are loveable and deserving of love, but in order to get love from others, you first have to love yourself. The love you show yourself will serve to show the people around you how to love you. Besides, how would you even know what love truly feels if you haven't first practicalized it on yourself?

Self-acceptance and self-love are the doorways to self-improvement. Until you accept and love yourself for who you are, you will never see those aspects of your life that need improvement because self-pity and self-regret will prevent you from discovering what you can truly improve on.

People who have great difficulty accepting and loving themselves for who they are most often spend their time trying to change who they are. Only through self-acceptance and self-love can you know the elements of your life that can be changed or improved and the aspects that can't.

Recognize and appreciate your individuality as it pertains to your identity since this is the first step toward living a life that is balanced, enjoyable, and satisfying. Nobody can give you what you haven't first given to yourself, so it would be in your best interest to accept and love who you are because you're all you've got.

Declare these words aloud:

- I accept and love myself for who God made me be
- I accept and love my complexion
- I accept and love my skin
- I accept and love my ethnicity
- I accept and love my race
- I accept and love my personality

- I accept and love my life
- I owe myself a daily dosage of love
- I will never deprive myself of this precious gift
- I accept and love everything about myself

Chapter 6
How to Eliminate the Feeling of "Not Good Enough"

"The commonest cause of insecurity in most people is self-comparison."

Affirmation: I am enough.

Self-comparison is one of the major inhibitors of self-expression. It has made so many people place themselves in the cocoon of self-dissatisfaction that it is making them believe they're not just good enough. It is only when you've understood that you're completely different and you're not anyone else that you'll start living life and enjoying it as you should.

You see people measuring themselves against others saying, why don't I have that? Oh, why is my life not like his? Why am I not that tall? Why is my nose not like his? Why is my skin not like others? Why am I this short? I wish I weren't black; maybe I would've... Oh, I wish I was from that family, maybe... etc.

These people completely take their eyes off themselves and focus on others who they think are better than they are. Listen, the only thing that self-comparison can do is to blind you from seeing who you really are and create the feeling of not being good enough.

Being enough is understanding who you are and accepting the fact that you're made perfect and complete. It is seeing yourself as an individual and embracing everything about your individuality. Nothing is missing in you, and you don't need to look a certain way or have certain things in your life to feel complete. You're already enough.

Some of us have an identity conflict, and we don't seem to know or understand who we are. We accept everything thrown at us by the media and start trying to fit the image the mainstream media are trying to make of us. We are trying to fit into someone else's idea of who we should be because we've allowed them to brainwash us into believing that something is missing in the way we look. We start feeling ashamed.

No one can make you feel complete or enough. Such a feeling stems from within based on your uniqueness as a person. If you have the feeling of not being enough, then you have to look deep within yourself to find what is causing such an awkward feeling in you and address it.

There's nothing as bad as trying to fit into another man's description of who he/she thinks you should for him/her to accept you as okay or complete. That is what conforming is all about; only someone that doesn't truly know and understand who he/she is conforms to other people's opinions.

Allowing anybody or anything to affect your identity or what you believe in is never wise. Not some stranger who knows nothing about you, but only you have the ability to choose what is acceptable and undesirable about yourself. Consider a circumstance in which you want to make modifications or enhancements to your physical appearance or personal characteristics. Such an upgrade or adjustment should be done because you believe it will enable you to enjoy a much better, higher quality of life than you already enjoy and not because you want to appear acceptable or good enough in the eyes of people who aren't concerned about your well-being.

Whatever you do for yourself should not be because you're trying to correct what you think is a defect, but because you know you deserve the best and want to make yourself the best you can be. Be confident and secure in your skin. Accepting, loving, and valuing yourself for who you are is essential. No one can make you feel good enough or adequate' and only you can make yourself feel that way.

There is nothing missing in you. You're complete, you're enough, and you should never entertain any thought or anyone that tells you otherwise. Yes, you are adequate! Yes, you're good enough! And it would be best if you always walked with this consciousness because you're the only one with the power to define who you are and make yourself feel good about yourself.

Declare these words aloud to yourself:

- I am made complete in all aspects

- I am enough in all aspects

- Everything about me is good

- Nothing is lacking or missing in m

- I will never wish to be like anyone else

- I will never allow my feelings or anyone to make me feel ashamed or less of myself

- I will always see and appreciate the awesome qualities in me

- I will never undermine myself in any way

- I know I am made complete

- I am good enough for the good things of life

Chapter 7
Take Responsibility for Your Life

"When you fail to do what you're supposed to do in order to make your life better, you're making the decision to settle for lesser than you deserve."

Affirmation: I refuse to settle for less.

Settling for less is living less than you're truly worth. And the majority of us are settling for less. We are living a life inferior to what we are worth. Why? We've made ourselves believe that we can't actually have what we deserve and have gotten fed up with not making any headway.

I see so many black kids dropping out of school and refusing to learn a skill, and I'm wondering about the type of life they desire for themselves and their children. Our girls are doing odd jobs and turning to stripping; one can't help but wonder the type of quality life that such girls live. What about our men/young men? Many of them are taking to drugs, crimes, and all sorts of harmful lifestyles, and we wonder why things aren't getting better for us.

Nothing is going to even work out until you put up the effort to make it work. If you want to see any genuine good development or change in your life, you must be the one who initiates and facilitates such progress or change. We are complaining that we are not being given opportunities, and we're being excluded from the economic opportunities in our country, but let me ask this: should an opportunity come your way now, will you actually be in a position to grasp it? Are you employable? Do you have a marketable skill? Do you have a degree? What do you have that you can use to earn an honest living and give yourself comfort in life?

Life is designed in a way that everything has its time and season. Have you ever sat down and considered if what you're presently doing can sustain you for as long as you desire and give you comfort in life? Is what you're currently doing making you feel good and proud of yourself? Are you living life or just trying to get by (survive)?

Your life is the product of all your decisions. Today's decisions and actions determine the quality of life you will live tomorrow. And most of us are making the decision to settle for less than we should be getting by choosing to do nothing about our future. We're placing ourselves in tight corners where people and life can easily use us.

Maybe some of us lack support; perhaps the system is in some way working against us; perhaps our community or neighborhoods are not inspiring us enough; maybe your color is making you be discriminated against, etc. Whatever your reason, it is not aspiring you to put in the effort to make yourself better. I just want to let you know that "you don't have an excuse!

There's no way you will make great decisions, take significant actions, and not have a great life. The majority of us are living a life of "less," not because we never had options but because we chose to take the easy way. We are giving ourselves excuses not to work hard for the type of life we truly desire.

We are ending up blaming everyone else for our uneventful life of struggle but ourselves. If you can't take responsibility for your life, you'll keep struggling at the bottom. Your life is your responsibility. Your success or failure is your responsibility. The building up of your life is your responsibility.

Nobody owes you anything: you owe yourself everything. If you really want to live a great life, you have to desire it and work hard for it. Failure means that you're making up your mind to settle for the crumbs that fall off life's table.

Your comfort in life is in your hands, and you have the ability to make your life as comfortable as you want it to be. So I'm asking you, "are you gonna settle and do what everyone else is doing or you're gonna go for the best?"

Declare these words aloud to yourself:

- My comfort in life is in my hands
- I can make my life as comfortable as I want it to be
- So I choose to make the best decisions and actions that will give me an edge in life
- I choose to take responsibility for my life
- I refuse to settle for less

Chapter 8
The Instigator of Confidence

"A man's belief in his/her seal of approval. Whatever you don't believe, you don't approve of, and whatever you don't approve of, you won't give it your all and thus cannot get it done."

Affirmation: I have confidence in my abilities.

One of the reasons some of us don't attain greater heights in life is because we don't believe we can attain such heights. You can never get anything done without considering that you have the ability to get it done. You can never effectively utilize a tool or gift if you don't have the confidence to put into use.

If you can't do something, it's not because you can't actually do it or suck at it, but because you've yet to believe that you have what it takes to do it. The ability to do anything you can imagine in life is within you, but you can never discover such an ability unless you first believe in it.

Your belief enables you to discover your ability and stir in yourself the confidence to do whatever it takes. I will take a moment to ask you this question: "who do you think you are?"

You will be as confident as the perception you have of yourself. What do you think about yourself? Do you think you're beneath others or above them? Do you think you have great talents and abilities? Or do you see yourself an empty vessel with nothing to offer?

Your confidence is the assurance that you have whatever it takes to accomplish what you set your mind on. It comes down to your belief in your abilities and yourself. It is the seal of approval that you are able and capable. It is the force that gets you to stand up and act.

Nobody can achieve anything in life without confidence. Extraordinary abilities or skills without confidence lead to mediocrity. All the great women and men you've heard about gave themselves an opportunity to be heard because they chose to ignore that voice of self-doubt that was preventing them from taking charge of the opportunities before them.

Discover your unique gifts, sharpen your skills, develop yourself, read widely, and equip yourself with all that gives you an incredible edge on the path you've chosen in life. When you know who you are and believe that you're capable of anything you set your mind on, you will never allow fear to silence you from taking action when you need to. Whenever an opportunity shows up to make the world know the stuff you're made of, don't chicken out or allow fear to shut you up. Stand up like the king you are and let the world know what you've got in you.

Be confident in yourself and never allow fear, anyone, or anything ever to stop you from expressing the beautiful gifts, talents, skills, and abilities that God has deposited in you. Only when you display your gifts can the people around you know your worth and feel compelled to give you a shot.

Believe in yourself, think you can get anything done, and activate the ability already deposited in you. Your confidence is in your belief, and when you believe you can, the confidence to make it happen will automatically spring from you.

Declare these words aloud to yourself:

- I will not allow fear to cause me to bottle up my skills, talents, and abilities

- I will not allow anyone stops me from expressing the kinds of stuff that I am made of

- I will be confident in myself

- In order to express myself, I will constantly hunt for opportunities to do so

- I will give myself a shot at life

- I will take my chances

- I believe in myself

- I have confidence in my abilities

- I have confidence in myself

Chapter 9
We all Need Good Counselors

"When you don't listen, the mistake will be inevitable."

Affirmation: I will listen to good counsel and instructions.

Some of the shits we go through in life could have been avoided if we had listened. Still, our pride, stubbornness, and foolishness always get in the way and compel us to resist and rebel against anyone that tries to tell us what's right or counsel us against certain actions we're taking or about to take that may ruin our lives if we don't retrace our steps.

I have seen young women and men that angrily left home because their parent(s) tried to question the sort of risky lifestyle they're choosing to live and tried to direct them on the right path to take. And most of these cases I have seen never end well for the child.

Sometimes, you can only see clearly and better with the eyes of other people: mostly the eyes of those around you that love you and truly got your back. When someone else tells you about your action and tries to counsel you about it, he/she isn't trying to control you or tell you how to live your life; he/she is just trying to make you see what you've been unable to see concerning such activities and it would be in your best interest to give their real concern consideration as no one knows it all.

You put yourself, your future, and your life at risk anytime you resist a counsel that is aimed to make you better or intends to open your eyes to see the danger in whatever it is that you're doing. Yeah, sometimes the counselor's approach may be wrong, but what is important is what they are saying or trying to make you see.

A man that has made costly mistakes in life or seen people around him make costly mistakes, and the grave consequences of such mistakes in the lives of its perpetrators would never want anyone close to him or that he truly cares about to be caught in the web of such same deadly mistakes.

Your parents or guardians are like the signpost that points you in the right direction in life: they can only point or direct you in the right direction, but going in that direction will be your sole decision.

I know that not all parents or guardians are playing their God-given roles in their kids' lives, as some of them are nowhere to be found. But if you're lucky to have parents or guardians that are doing such, you'd better consider yourself lucky; sit yourself down, put aside your stubbornness and pride, and tap from their wisdom.

I need to let you know here that no parent is perfect. Our parents or guardians are humans like us with flaws too. They are not super humans but mere humans like you. But they have experiences and knowledge that would help guide you on the right path in life if you would listen to them and adhere to their good counsel and guidance.

Some of us make the mistake of judging our parents or guardian by their mistakes and refuse to follow their wise counsels and guidance because of such mistakes. Look, you put yourself, your life, and your future in danger when you resist the wise counsel and guidance of your parents, guardians, or anyone that truly have your interest at heart.

You need to understand that the counsels and guidance that you're being given are for your good. These counsels will always come in handy when you need to make your own choices in life.

Love your parents, never challenge their authority over you and pay attention to their good counsel. When your parents act emotional and yell sometimes, or when they try to compel you to do certain things, it's not because they like yelling or they want to prove to you that they have the power to compel you to do their biddings; it's because they're seeing you heading toward a path that will be destructive to you and they want to make you understand that there's destruction lurking around such path.

Your parents love you, and they want the best for you. Listen to their good counsel and follow their guidance. If you turn out to be someone great tomorrow, they will share in the glory, and if you choose to rebel and choose the wrong path, they will also share in the shame.

Sometimes, our parents can get on our nerves, but they are still our parents. So respect and listen to them and ensure that you choose a path in life that makes them proud always to tell anyone that cares to listen, "that is my son!"

Declare these words aloud to yourself:

- I will pay attention to good counsels;
- I will listen to wise instructions; and
- I will choose my paths wisely.
- I will not ever make the mistakes of my parents.

Chapter 10
The True Test of the Value of Your Desire

"The worth of your desire is measured by the obstacles you passed through to have it. If it was just so easy, everyone would have done it or gotten it, but the fact that everyone could not do it or have it should tell you that it is worth something."

Affirmation: I will not give up on myself.

Anything that is important to your wellbeing, your comfort, your future, and your life is worth fighting for. How bad you want it will determine how seriously you will go after it and how eager you will be to have it. You can only lose in life when you choose to give up on yourself, and nobody can make you give up on yourself – only you can.

How does a man that has given up on himself behave?

He would stop trying to make himself better; he would allow what people say or do to him prevent him from striving further; he would allow his challenges to compel him to involve himself in acts that may cost him his freedom or life, he would lose confidence in himself and his abilities; he would start living his life carelessly and without direction, etc.

When you give up on yourself, you will deprive yourself of having a shot at giving yourself the best in life. The road towards one's success is not always a smooth one, and you must be prepared to deal with the bumps, potholes, speed-breakers, and barriers that you will come across on your path.

You will make mistakes, you will fall here and there, people will get in your way and try to prevent you from expressing yourself, some people won't even give you a chance, and some will tell you that you don't have what it takes, etc. All these they would do in a bid to break you down and prevent you from having what you have the ability for and truly deserve.

Don't allow them to break you, and don't be the one to break yourself. Don't believe any lie that anyone will tell you about yourself, and don't give up on yourself. Nothing good comes easy, and anything that is worthwhile is worth fighting for. Believe in your abilities, belief in yourself, and make a resolve to never give up on yourself until you get the change that you seek.

The trial is just temporary. If you will keep your head up, never give up on yourself and resolve in your heart to make your life count, you will certainly overcome it and attain your heart desires.

Declare these words aloud to yourself:

- Regardless of what I go through in life,
- I will never give up on myself until I get the change I seek.
- I will go for what I desire with all that I've got;
- When I fall, I will pick myself up;
- I will face my fears;
- I will fight my battles;
- I will win the war; and
- I will claim my trophy;
- I will never give up.

Chapter 11
Use It to Your Advantage

"The easiest way to get unnoticed is to be like everyone else."

Affirmation: I appreciate my differences and uniqueness.

Being different is a good thing. It makes you easily seen and stand out from the crowd. Imagine someone different from everyone else being exceptional at whatever he does, and such a person will easily get noticed and talked about by everyone.

I think it's high time we start using our differences to our advantage. A situation in which I was one of the very few black students or members of a group would be a wonderful chance for me to work even harder and become one of the top students or members of the group in question. That way, I easily get noticed and talked about.

Some people may feel threatened or intimidated by you and your exceptional performance, but that is a good thing. It's good for you to make them feel threatened and insecure around you with your exceptional performance or personality than for them to make you feel threatened because you think you can't measure up.

I must tell you this: there's a unique way you feel when you're very good at what you do in a place when you're the minority. You command attention and respect easily, and everyone gets scared to mess with you because they know that you're the real deal.

Have you noticed that most people of other races - mostly the racist ones feel very uncomfortable in the presence of a successful black person or a well exposed and educated black person, and they try to comport themselves when around such a black person? Look, you have to understand that your being different is a plus to you. The fact that you are actually in the limelight provides an excellent chance for you to demonstrate your abilities and make others realize that you are the genuine thing by showcasing your individuality and bragging about your achievements.

We should stop holding back and start going all out for what we want in life. Wherever we find ourselves, we should strive to be among the best. Our total liberation is in our excellence. No one can attempt to single us out negatively and talk down on us if they know that they can't measure up to us in anything. Just imagine us owning industries and calling some of the big shots in society. Do you think anyone would want to mess with such people?

We have everything in us to rise above our challenges and make ourselves heard and seen. Our differences have already placed us in an advantaged position, but we have to see them and exploit them. I know they are fighting so hard to ensure that we don't rise and manifest our greatness, but no one can keep a great man that doesn't want to be down on the ground for too long.

Most of our people have risen from obscurity to the limelight even with the many oppression, subjugation, deprivation, and economic alienation that people of our kind are being subjected to. You, too, can do it. You, too, can make a difference. You, too, can get yourself seen and heard – not for something terrible but for something outstanding.

The tide is beginning to change, and more and more opportunities are beginning to be made available for us. So we have to take such chances - not just take them but excel in them and make them understand that we genuinely deserve being given a shot.

You and I are placed in a unique position, and we can use that position to make ourselves seen and heard by choosing to be exceptional. We have it in us, and we shouldn't be scared to manifest the greatness we have in us wherever we find ourselves.

You were not designed to be the same as everyone else, and you were formed in a unique way as well. You were born with the ability to be extraordinary. You were made to be different from the rest of the pack. You were designed to be exceptional and to command respect wherever you are. You are unique! Everything about you is unique and interesting. You're unmatched. Accept your individuality and learn to use it to your advantage.

Be proud of your uniqueness because it is the symbol of your peculiarity. Don't ever wish to be like anyone else or strive to be like anyone else. You lose your uniqueness once you do that. You were created differently, and you were created special. So use your individuality to your advantage.

Declare these words aloud to yourself:

- I was created to be different;
- I was created to be unique;
- I was designed to stand out;
- I was created to be unique, and
- I intend to take use of my individuality to my benefit.

Chapter 12
You Deserve It

"If you don't take it, it may never be given to you. But you may never attempt to take it unless you believe that you truly deserve it. Also, if you believe you deserve it, you would go for it and do everything you can to have it."

Affirmation: I am worthy of every good thing that life has to offer.

Sometimes we take BS from people because we think we don't deserve to be respected or treated nicely. Some of us also settle for mediocrity and never wish to do anything about it because we think that's the level of life that we truly deserve. Listen, brother: no one will give you anything that you don't first think or believe you deserve.

How you go about your life and what you aim for in life is a reflection of what you believe your value is. Value is a personal thing as only you can create it. Your values influence what you accept from people and how you allow them to treat you.

Value is created in your mind. It is your belief of your worth. Your worth is what you think you deserve, and it is shown in your aspirations, words, decisions, and actions. When you know your worth, you don't take shit from people or life or settle; you go for the best.

And man, you are very valuable, and you deserve every good thing that life has to offer. Nobody is more worthy than you or deserves better treatment than you. You deserve the best in life, and you should always go for the best.

Living a good life is not the privilege of any race. Being comfortable in life is not any race's privilege. The top sphere of life is not reserved for any race – rather, it is reserved for the individual that can pay the price to get there.

Life is what you make of it, and you can have the kind of life you wish for if you can equip yourself with the tools, you need to make it possible and go for it with all that you've got in you.

Do all you can to have and give yourself the best in life because you deserve it. Don't ever deprive yourself of any good thing (or treatment) that you desire, and never ever allow anyone to deprive you of something good that you've truly worked for or deserve. You're the best, and you deserve to have the best. So don't ever settle for mediocrity because you're worthy of good treatment and every good thing that life has to offer.

Declare these words aloud to yourself:

- I know I am valuable.
- And I deserve to be respected.
- I deserve good treatment.
- because I am worthy of them all.
- The good things of life are also my privilege, and I will have them and enjoy them.

Chapter 13
The Choice is Yours to Make

"The decisions you make in life determine the quality of life you'll live."

Affirmation: I will choose my path wisely.

Everything you will become in life is tied to what is called "choice." The choice is your ability to choose. Your ability to know what is right, what you want to do with your life, and doing all you can to get it done.

Whether good or bad, right or wrong, education or illiteracy, working or staying idle, freedom or imprisonment, love or hate, crime or law-abiding, responsibility or irresponsibility, failure or success, etc., you're the one that will live with the consequences.

The kind and quality of life you lead will be determined by the quality of the decisions you make now. Where you are presently is a function of your past choices, and where you will be tomorrow or in the future will be a function of your today's choices and subsequent future choices.

Your choices are what determine the direction and outcomes of your life. If you make them wrongly, you're the one that will live with the consequences, and if you make them rightly, you're also the one that will enjoy the benefits. However you choose to make it, you will be the one in the center of it.

Therefore, you must proceed with carefully while making judgments, as they will determine how high you will soar or how far you will plummet in your professional and personal life. Always think through anything you intend to do and consider its pros and cons before carrying it out.

I am telling you this because most times, we are the ones that enslave ourselves with our actions. Getting yourself involved with bad company or engaging in any self-destructive act is a wrong path. Don't just let anybody persuade you to do anything that might jeopardize your freedom, your future, or your life.

Always keep an eye on yourself and keep an eye on your surroundings. Always ask yourself before involving yourself in anything or carrying out any act, "what's at stake?" Never allow anyone to push you into doing anything with serious consequences that may destroy your future or life.

Don't let regret be your companion. So many brothers are in prison, so many have lost their lives, so many have put themselves in tight corners and very difficult situations because of their choices. Don't make yourself one of such brothers.

Watch your steps. Watch your lifestyle. Watch your association. Many black people today are endangering themselves, their future, their freedom, and their lives because of the sort of dangerous lifestyle they're choosing to live. Don't put yourself in a tight situation and make regret your companion. You have an option. Only you can choose the path of your life, and the path you choose is what will be used to judge you by others, so I urge you to choose it wisely.

Declare these words aloud to yourself:

- I will be careful with my decisions;
- I will be careful with my actions;
- I will be careful with my choices;
- I will choose my path wisely;
- I will never gamble with my life.

Chapter 14
Affirmations for Self-Esteem

People who have no self-esteem often think that they will become confident and happy with themselves when their current situation changes. Seeing a beautiful face when you look into the mirror will make you walk with your shoulders high up, having caring parents will make you feel normal and happy, scoring all A's in your exam will enable you to look your classmates in the eye and say whatever you want, your neighbors will respect you when you own a car and that will boost your confidence, getting married will elevate your status and in turn, make you feel less inferior about yourself.

Self-esteem or the lack thereof is related to external circumstances. "If A or B happens, my self-esteem will increase," so they think. While it is possible that you will see yourself in a better light and get a sense of self-worth from achieving great things, that level of highness you feel will most likely not last. Why? Self-esteem is basically a state of mind. Although the current state of your life and other people's opinion of you may have a bearing on your self-esteem, the ultimate determinant of your self-esteem is your thoughts.

Take this scenario, for instance, and Unemployed Miss A thinks Miss B, who is employed, is more intelligent and better than she is. Employed Miss B tells herself that she would have been running her own business by now if only she was as smart and efficient as her entrepreneur friend. Then there is Miss C, who is also unemployed but thinks her situation is not a result of her not being good enough but because she is yet to develop the skills needed for the job.

What differentiates Miss C from both Miss A and Miss B? The way she sees herself. Miss C understands that she doesn't possess the skills that will land her the job she wants but instead of thinking there is something inherently wrong with her, she singles out the problem and separates it from her core being.

Between Miss C and Miss B, who do you think lives a happy life? It's Miss C, of course. As humans, we are aware of our identity: hating the way we look, how we act, or the family we come from automatically cripples our sense of self-worth. Your level of self-esteem usually depends on how much you like and appreciate yourself.

Don't confuse healthy self-esteem with too high or 'overly inflated' self-esteem, though. Thinking you are superior to everybody is just as psychologically unhealthy as seeing yourself as the dust of the earth—the worst being on earth, undeserving of love. You overestimate your abilities, praise yourself too much, and expect others to do the same even when you don't deserve it. Other people are seen through a diminishing lens, and you act as though the world revolves around you.

Having self-esteem that is too high is dangerous and damaging, especially because it prevents you from embracing self-improvement.

Self-esteem is more complicated than the popular 'high vs. low' concept that is often used to describe it. If you say you have high self-esteem, does it mean you never have moments of self-doubt? And for those who think they have low self-esteem, has there never been a time you felt proud or good about yourself? Given the fact that sentiments change, it might be difficult to determine your degree of self-esteem with certainty. One minute you feel so good about yourself, and the next minute, you are plagued with self-doubt.

Being the human that you are, it is normal to experience varying feelings—both positive and negative. In order to fully benefit from this book, measuring your self-esteem by taking the following self-esteem checkup will be extremely helpful. Be honest as you can when answering the questions. The answers you give will help you recognize how you esteem yourself.

Everybody has a measure of self-esteem, and the level of self-esteem you have now has a source. Our childhood, that innocent period when we didn't know our left from our right when we were led by the hands and guided by our parents and other grown-ups in our lives, is usually a major decisive factor of our self-esteem.

You didn't know that touching fire could burn the skin until your parents told you. Talking loudly, eating while you talk, sitting with your legs spread wide in a panties-revealing way as a girl, not combing your hair, not brushing your teeth every morning, mingling with your unruly neighbors, collecting something from a stranger, or running around in the streets are some behaviors your parents probably told you to desist from doing.

Parents who model self-esteem know how to get their kids to do the right thing while also respecting the individuality and opinions of their children. They encourage you, consistently show you, love, back you up when necessary, and make you understand in a clear and reasonable way how they expect you to behave. These types of parents make sure it sinks in that it is your behavior that is bad, not you as a human being.

Authoritarian parents or permissive parents, on the other hand, usually have a poor way of using words as they tend to be less concerned about the feelings or mental growth of their children. "Stop littering the floor, dirty child," they say, or "bad child, you can never do anything right." Each inappropriate behavior you display earns you doses of scolding or spanking. Some parents nowadays even go to the extent of pushing their kids away or denying them something essential to their existence like food or school fees when their children misbehave.

Consciously or unconsciously, you know that your survival depends on your parents as a child. Their approval matters a lot to you as you don't want to lose their support. Automatically, you start thinking of yourself as a bad, useless or lazy person when you find yourself staying till nightfall without brushing your teeth, hanging out with your 'unruly' neighbors, talking loudly, or doing some other thing that you often receive punishment for doing.

All of these feelings seep into your teenage and adulthood, inflicting your self-esteem. You will find yourself constantly struggling to unlearn what you were often told was the best way to behave or the standard form of elegance.

It all reverts back to thoughts, no matter where your self-esteem stems from parents, traumatic experience, or negative peers; one major factor binds all your feelings and your sense of self-worth together: your thoughts. You should put effort towards challenging your debasing, embarrassing, or painful thoughts.

Although, when a child is always told that he or she is ugly, lazy, and stingy, or dull, he or she grows up with a nagging sense of wrongness. It becomes hard to work to be convinced otherwise. Fortunately, building healthy self-esteem can only be difficult, not impossible.

For what reasons should you devote your time and energy to boosting your own self-esteem? Your overall health and performance depend on it. When you judge and reject yourself, you bring pain upon yourself. Life becomes unexciting, and you engage in activities that are harmful to your health. It is not uncommon to find people struggling with their self-esteem abusing alcohol and drugs, eating poorly, becoming promiscuous, enduring abusive relationships, or suffering from psychosomatic illnesses like indigestion, headache, fatigue, and insomnia.

As you think that people will hate you or not want to associate with you, you withdraw from social settings and end up feeling lonely. Anxiety, stress symptoms, and depression are usually the accompanying baggage of poor self-esteem. Your performance at school and work also bears the brunt of your self-esteem. In the absence of healthy self-esteem, fear overshadows the drive to seize and maximize opportunities for growth.

The fear of self-rejection and judgment makes you take fewer academic, career, or social risks. You already believe that you won't succeed, not when people who are better than you are around, so you shy away from job interviews or meeting people.

Living with a negative sense of self-worth prevents you from maximizing your full potential as it limits your ability to ask for help, handle criticism, express yourself, and solve problems. It's like being your own prisoner, you have an idea that you are capable of achieving so much more, but since you are locked behind the gate of unbelief and fear, you remain stagnant.

With healthy self-esteem comes the ability to navigate life with an assertive and positive attitude –to be truly free from the cage of perfectionism, poor perception of self, and self-rejection. You can stop the judgments and change the way you feel about yourself.

The Affirmations

1. I have the ability to accomplish anything that I set my mind to.

2. I believe that my future is bright and that things will work out for the best for me.

3. I believe in myself and my abilities.

4. I triumph over my mistakes.

5. I learn from each experience to improve myself and do better next time.

6. I radiate positive energy, and my unwavering enthusiasm helps benefit others.

7. I have an engaging and warm personality that draws people to want to be around me.

8. I have the conviction to follow through on my beliefs.

9. I celebrate my uniqueness and individuality instead of comparing myself to others.

10. I am confident and secure in myself no matter what others think.

11. I possess the confidence to take charge of my own life.

12. I am generous and giving, and take other people's best interest into consideration.

13. I prioritize my long term happiness over instant gratification.

14. The capacity to make the right decisions is something in which I have great trust and confidence.

15. I am at my best when I think happy thoughts and push negative emotions to the side.

16. When I believe in myself, I perform at my highest level.

17. I am at my best when I persevere to finish the task before me.

18. I motivate and encourage others to believe in themselves.

19. Whenever I see someone who has achieved something that I want, I see it as inspiration and evidence that I can achieve the same.

20. I conquer my fears and turn them into strengths.

21. I deserve happiness and success because I am a good person.

22. Regardless of my ambitions, I pursue my goals with morality and ethics.

23. I value myself as a person because I have strong character traits of honesty and integrity.

24. I participate in activities that I enjoy to bring happiness into my life.

25. I gladly take on challenges to further increase my self-confidence and boost my self-esteem.

26. I confront my personal demons and turn them around with self-awareness and positive action.

27. I love doing kind things for others because it makes us both happier.

28. I treat myself kindly because I know I am worthy of respect.

29. I love and appreciate what my body does for me, so I pay attention to what I feed it.

30. I possess skills and talents that other people could benefit from.

31. I possess the will and the resourcefulness to change things in my life for the better.

32. I am an authentic and genuine person, capable of speaking my mind fearlessly.

33. I treat others with respect and surround myself with people who treat me with respect.

34. I am a beautiful person, and I respect myself by taking care of my body and my mind.

35. I possess the stamina and endurance to persevere in my pursuits.

36. I am confident and assertive at all times regardless of what other people may think.

37. On a continual basis, I am learning more about myself and working to improve my areas of weaker performance.

38. I deserve to feel happy because I'm worth it and I matter.

39. Before I can love others, I must first learn to truly and fully love and appreciate myself.

40. I make it a priority to be kind to myself.

41. I have control over my effort, and always put my best foot forward.

42. I take care of my outer appearance because the confidence that causes makes me feel better on the inside.

43. I have the willpower to take a break from outside influences like social media if I find myself comparison shaming.

44. My opinion matters, even if it is unpopular.

45. I have the courage to speak my mind on subjects that are important to me.

46. The way I see others is a reflection of the way I see myself.

47. I am better because of the tight knit bonds I have with my friends and family.

48. I feel attractive and confident.

49. I walk into every room with a confident posture.

50. I constantly take note of my talents and abilities to remind myself that I am capable of accomplishing anything.

51. I take time to celebrate my achievements and highlight my successes.

52. I am a loyal and genuine person, and anyone would be lucky to have a relationship with me.

53. The capacity to make others laugh and grin is something I have. I have a fantastic sense of humor.

54. I care for my body with consistent physical exercise because it makes me feel positive about myself.

55. I am a selfless and generous person.

56. I take time to volunteer to help those less fortunate than me.

57. I forgive others because the act of forgiveness is empowering.

58. I possess the potential and the drive to succeed, and I am worthy of success.

59. I am the kind of person who is destined for success and greatness.

60. I speak kind words to myself and remind myself that I can do well and succeed.

61. I evaluate my progress and success based on what I am doing, not what other people are doing.

62. I achieve tiny victories every day that I celebrate and commend myself for.

63. I value myself enough to choose to spend time only with people who love me for who I am.

64. I accept myself as I am, with all of my flaws, and I strive to better myself on a daily basis.

65. I channel all negativity and turn it into something positive.

66. I possess the courage to keep trying even if I do not succeed the first time around.

67. I have the self-discipline to deliver on all of my promises.

68. My self-esteem allows me to reflect on my previous triumphs and motivate me towards new accomplishments.

69. I have limitless potential to succeed and become the best version of myself.

70. I always come out a stronger and better person when I face and overcome adversity.

71. I focus on the present and improving myself for the future, rather than dwelling on the past.

72. I always cultivate feelings of gratitude.

73. I stay mindful of all the happiness I have in my life.

74. I wake up excited every morning, grateful to live another day.

75. I am grateful for the opportunity to become my best self and live my best life.

76. The messages my body, mind and stomach are sending me are constantly in sync with each other.

77. I set aside personal time to engage in activities I enjoy because it makes me feel happy.

78. My space is an expression of who I am, and it reflects my individuality, and my cheerful mood.

79. I proudly display personal items and awards in my space that remind me of my accomplishments.

80. I am enthusiastic about life, which fuels my motivation.

81. I am strong in my will, and I am able to overcome any temporary setbacks.

82. I constantly put effort into becoming happy on the inside because I know that turns into success on the outside.

83. I possess strong desire and determination—two key factors in creating success.

84. I confidently and happily invest in myself because I know I have what it takes to succeed.

85. I have a positive and inclusive worldview.

86. I am accepting of all people's differences, choices, and opinions.

87. I am proud of my positive personal attributes.

88. I always keep my past achievements at top of mind to keep myself encouraged.

89. An optimistic attitude is part of my identity.

90. I am brave and determined enough to keep pushing forward, even through difficult times.

91. I deserve the opportunity to have a rich, fulfilling life.

92. I have excellent critical thinking and problem solving abilities that serve me well in my life and work.

93. I take control over transforming my life because I believe in myself.

94. My positive thinking contributes to positive growth.

95. I have the dignity and self-confidence to always be true to myself.

96. I am proud of my individual uniqueness, as that is what defines me and makes me special.

97. I have a gift of finding the bright side in every situation.

98. My sunny disposition constantly attracts people who improve the quality of my life.

99. I am constantly making progress in my emotional control, emotional development, and emotional intelligence.

100. I have the conviction that my dreams are worthwhile and should be pursued.

101. I am dedicated enough to put forth maximum effort until I become successful.

102. I have the self-control to reject any unhealthy impulses.

103. I have the maturity to see people and situations purely for what they are, and not take anything personally.

104. I am a positive role model for myself and others.

105. I am an optimistic person, with an optimistic mind, heart, and spirit.

106. I have the willpower to resist temptations that do not help me become the best version of myself.

107. I only compare myself to myself and not to others.

108. I have the courage to do the right thing in any situation.

109. I have the power to control my own level of happiness.

110. I love and accept myself, and it inspires others around me to do the same.

111. I remain encouraged and persist with a positive attitude in the face of difficulty.

112. I have the courage to take risks and put myself out there.

113. I have the strength of character to let small things go and always be the bigger person.

114. I am the gatekeeper of my own mind, and I only grant access to positivity.

115. I have the will to change my circumstances when things are not going well.

116. When I want something different, I have the willpower to do something different.

117. I deserve to have hopes and dreams to pursue.

118. I am certain that happiness and success are in my future.

119. I have the patience required to make continuous life improvements.

120. I am a good-natured person, and I do not allow negativity to drag me down.

121. I have the self-compassion to not be overly critical of myself.

122. I am comfortable with giving and receiving compliments and praise.

123. I am secure enough to discuss my viewpoints and experiences with my peers without shame or fear of judgment.

124. I have the individuality to make my own decisions and take responsibility for them.

125. I have valuable opinions to contribute, and I share them with others.

126. Success is not something that's just for others, it is for me.

127. Success is within my control and within my grasp.

128. I am worthy and deserving of all the great things life has in store for me.

129. I am fully equipped to create my version of an ideal life.

130. I have talents and abilities that will get me to where I need to go.

131. I can and I will rise to the top.

132. I am just as capable and deserving of success as anyone else is.

133. I choose to give more attention to my strengths than my weaknesses.

134. My high self-esteem allows me to build strong, long-lasting personal and professional relationships.

135. I am at peace with who I am inside and out.

136. I incorporate physical and mental practices into my daily life that promote positivity and combat negativity.

137. I have the resolve to keep growing and bettering myself every day.

138. I am worthy of being loved by people romantically and platonically.

139. I have the willpower to reshape my thoughts into an optimistic outlook.

140. I proudly and boldly create my own unique identity and don't care what other people think about me.

Chapter 15
Affirmations for Self-Love

You are loved. The universe often conspires against you. In many aspects of life, you are despised. Self-hatred is frequently instilled in children at a young age, along with a desire to be someone or something other than who the Lord has created you to be. Despite the fact that hate has attempted to destroy you, you continue to rise. You are cherished by your Creator, black guy. Your moms, sisters, cousins, brothers, and dads all adore you. Perhaps they are unable to do so because they lack the necessary knowledge. Maybe it's because we don't know how to accept true love when it's provided. Even yet, the truth remains that you are dearly loved. And the love you have the ability to give may break through barriers. The love you have the ability to give may offer peace, bridges, and longer tables, as well as healing, joy, and restoration. Give love whenever you can. Model adoration. Your love has the power to dispel a great deal of hatred.

In fact, self-love is the most rewarding sort of love, owing to the fact that it not only helps you to achieve more for yourself (which is both wonderful and powerful), but it also allows you to draw more into your life from other people. Love is a high-vibrational magnetic force, and your shift in energy will attract individuals who have a similar vibrational frequency to you.

Self-love affirmations are only one of the tools you may use to help you feel better about yourself and earn greater self-acceptance. What's the greatest part? They are the most straightforward strategy you can use in your life to foster more self-acceptance!

These affirmations for self-love may be utilized on a daily basis, and with continued usage, you can anticipate to experience increased happiness, confidence, joy, and other positive emotions. You'll increase your self-esteem, recognize that you are deserving of love, let go of negative ideas and welcome in compassion, have more constant positive thoughts, and strengthen your relationships with yourself and others as a result.

The Affirmations

1. I am whole and entire just the way I am.
2. Everything that I need is within me.
3. I am wholly secure in my being my best self.
4. Today, I choose to let go of any negative thoughts, feelings, and impulses that may circulate within me.
5. Today, I am fully committed to choosing the best version of myself.
6. I have unique gifts, talents, and skills.
7. I am enough.
8. From this moment forward, I fully commit to believing in myself and my gifts.
9. I have a unique personality that brings joy to those around me.
10. I have a special divine purpose that only I can fulfill.
11. I love the person that I am currently and the person that I am becoming.
12. My life is a source of love and happiness.
13. I am stepping into abundance in every single area of my life.
14. I am not defined by my mistakes.

15. I am made better by the mistakes I have made in my past.

16. My identity is not defined by my worst moments. Nor is it defined by my best moments.

17. I am far more than the sum of my failures or successes.

18. My identity stems from a source of energy more powerful than I could ever imagine.

19. I hereby choose to totally let go of all of fears in my spirit.

20. I am growing every single day, and for that I am enough.

21. I am learning every single day, and for that, I am enough.

22. I am doing my best to become my best every single day, and for that, I am enough.

23. I am much more than the outward manifestation of my body.

24. My value lies in something much deeper than my outer appearance.

25. What I look like on the outside is not who I am.

26. My image inside radiates outside.

27. I am beautiful outside because I am beautiful inside, not the other way around.

28. I am undeniably worthy of love and peace.

29. I am undeniably worthy of all the great things this life has to offer.

30. My spirit is free and unchained.

31. I hold all of my accomplishments and failures with equal emotion because I am defined by neither.

32. I wholly accept who I am and the person that I am becoming.

33. Mine is the only acceptance and approval that will ever be needed in my life.

34. I radiate positivity and loving energy to all that I come in contact with.

35. I am fully loved by myself and others.

36. I am fully love-able by myself and others even when it doesn't feel like it.

37. I am wonderful, inside and out.

38. I have the inherent freedom to make any choices that I wish.

39. I carry the intellect, wisdom and inner power to freely choose what I believe is best for me.

40. I am open to signs of guidance that come my way because I know I do not know all the answers.

41. I easily accept compliments and just as easily give them to those around me.

42. I choose to never take anything personally.

43. I hereby choose to always do my absolute best.

44. I only speak the very best of myself.

45. I only speak the very best of others.

46. I do not make negative assumptions about those around me.

47. I am wanted and desired.

48. I honor my values in all ways at all times.

49. I refuse to sacrifice my core values in favor of what may feel good at the moment.

50. I am always moving closer to self-mastery.

51. I show love for others as freely as I show love for myself.

52. I am not held back by any shame from my past.

53. I unashamedly share my talents and achievements with others.

54. I will make certain that I achieve and maintain all of my physical objectives since I am deserving of it.

55. I have no constraints or limits on my dreams.

56. I choose to celebrate who I am now and who I am becoming in the future.

57. It is never too late to follow my aspirations, and I believe this to be true.

58. I have everything I need to make my life into what I want it to be.

59. I am a success. Period.

60. I am overflowing with love for others because I have so much love for myself.

61. I am confidently and excitedly moving forward into the next phase of my life.

62. I am worthy of praise and admiration from others.

63. I have the power to heal physically, mentally, and emotionally from anything.

64. The only thing that defines my success is my willingness to persevere and move forward.

65. I am filled with gratitude for my circumstances and blessings.

66. I love myself to bring my authentic being everywhere I go.

67. The best expression of self-love is how I care for my body inside and out.

68. I carry sufficient strength for fighting through any adversity that confronts me.

69. I am a physical incarnation of love and light.

70. I choose to live my life with exuberance and enthusiasm.

71. I give myself the approval that I crave from others.

72. I deserve love the way that I am right now.

73. I show myself how much I love myself by the quality of self-talk I engage in.

74. I choose to tell myself good things because I love myself.

75. I am always getting closer to fulfilling my destiny and becoming the very best that I can be.

76. My personal journey has pushed me towards all of the gifts and joys that are in front of me.

77. I am now loving myself in a deeper way than I have ever loved myself before.

78. I am constantly gaining more and more clarity and peace.

79. What is being impressed within me is beginning to be expressed around me.

80. My best attributes far outweigh my worst.

81. I possess a deep love for myself and my body.

82. There is nothing that can hold me back from being the best expression of my true self.

83. I am connected to the strongest source of power in the universe.

84. My connection to universal power lifts me high above my circumstances.

85. I carry the power to change my circumstances and achieve all of my goals.

86. My mind and body are working together to help me reach my full potential.

87. I have so much in my life that is worthy of celebration and enjoyment.

88. It is now my time to shine.

89. Self-confidence, harmony, and peace of mind come naturally to me.

90. I love everything about my appearance.

91. As I practice self-love, I become more capable of being loved.

92. I live my truth.

93. I live my life unashamed of my weaknesses.

94. Even when I feel weak, I am still strong.

95. My struggles are nothing but opportunities for growth.

96. I am not a prisoner to my circumstances.

97. My heart is healed from the hurt of my past.

98. I love myself enough to step forward and embrace new adventures that will help me to grow.

99. I make strides daily to become a better version of who I am.

100. I let go of past rejections.

101. Rejection does not have a say in who I am.

102. Rejection does not have a say in what I deserve.

103. Rejection does not have a say in what I am capable of.

104. I am capable of communicating with confidence and certainty.

105. My spirit is an infinite ocean of calm.

106. Serenity is embedded deep within me.

107. No matter what, I am at peace with my past.

108. No matter what, I am at peace with my present.

109. No matter what, I am at peace with my future.

110. I will always believe in myself even if no one else does.

111. I love myself and every aspect of who I am.

112. I am proud of the person I want to be and the progress I have made.

113. Day by day, minute by minute, I grow to love more of my life and everything in it.

114. I have the power and confidence to chase my dreams with fervor and passion.

115. I will always be there for myself, regardless of what I go through.

116. I find peace and joy in my moments of solitude because I love my own company.

117. I am far too much a gift for the world to carry any feelings of self-pity.

118. I will never be alone because I will always be there for myself.

119. I have an unshakeable inner strength.

120. There is much more to me than what it seems from the outside.

121. I am excited about my potential and how it will positively influence my future.

122. I am always finding new reasons to appreciate my uniqueness.

123. Each and every day, I choose to be the very best that I can possibly be.

124. I have confidence in my capacity to make choices that will lead to my financial well-being.

125. I embrace every opportunity to grow as a person and maximize everything that I can be.

126. I am whole, I am complete, and I am worthy.

127. I love the process of becoming my best self.

128. I am in love with identifying the areas of myself that I can improve upon.

129. I am worth more than any words I could ever use to describe me.

130. I hold unlimited power inside of me.

131. Wonder exist within me in abundance.

132. Every step I take is taken with courage and love for myself.

133. I celebrate my many victories and expect to have many more.

134. I am a bright, shining beacon of love.

135. I am worthy of compassion and kindness.

136. I am worthy of endless affection from others.

137. Nothing can diminish the love that I have for myself.

138. I am simply wonderful.

139. Happiness is always accessible to me.

140. I can always make the choice to love myself.

141. I make decisions that are in my best interest.

142. All of my decisions reflect the love and respect that I have for myself.

143. I openly acknowledge and share my gifts and talents.

144. Because I love myself, I am open to improving my weaknesses without self-judgment.

145. My love for myself prevents me from succumbing to external pressures.

146. My self-love instills a strong foundation of faith in myself.

147. I am patient with others because I am patient with myself.

148. When confronted with hate, my heart is immediately filled with love.

149. I honor my unique talents by sharing them with the world.

150. I love myself enough to be assertive when needed.

151. I love myself enough to speak my truth at all times.

152. I am centered and grounded in who I am.

153. I am powerful beyond all measure in pursuit of my dreams.

154. I move through life in complete peace and calm.

155. My life is centered on showing love for all people including myself.

156. I consistently do my best, every time.

157. I love myself enough to have a strong motivation within me to succeed.

158. I exercise grace for the benefit of myself and others.

159. I have complete trust in who I am and what I am capable of.

160. I love myself enough to never stop working towards my goals until I achieve them.

161. I always continue pushing forward, even though the worst of storms, because what is on the other side is worth it.

162. My heart is full of love for myself and others.

163. I always stand up for myself.

164. I am worthy of all new and incredible opportunities that life has to offer.

165. I love my past failures because of the lessons they have taught me to make me better.

166. I draw from my past only when it makes my present better.

167. I lovingly embrace my flaws because it is a part of what makes me unique.

168. I lovingly embrace my strengths because it is a part of what makes me unique.

169. I equally embrace my strengths and my weaknesses, as they collectively make up who I am.

170. I have the power to change the parts of myself that I do not like.

171. I practice self-care as a way to enhance my self-love.

172. Taking great care of my body is one of the ways that I show myself love.

173. I approve of who I am.

174. I take pride in my past.

175. I release all thoughts or beliefs that are not aligned with love for myself.

176. I take action on improving the parts of my body that I can control.

177. I lovingly embrace and accept the parts of my body that I cannot control.

178. I take action on improving the parts of my appearance that I can control.

179. I lovingly embrace and accept the parts of my appearance that I cannot control.

180. My view of myself is the only one that truly matters.

181. I have a loving view of myself that cannot be disparaged by external forces.

182. I have a loving view of myself that is strong enough to withstand anything other people might say.

183. Other people don't have to love me in order for me to love myself.

184. I affirm and grow my self-love through repeated positive self-talk.

185. Regardless of what it looks like, my body works the way it should, and for that I am grateful.

186. I fully trust my conscience to show me the right way.

187. I will not be defined by anything negative that was said about me in my past.

188. I determine my value, not others.

189. My self-worth is in my own hands, not in the hands of others.

190. I forgive myself for any past behavior I committed that was not in alignment with self-respect.

191. Every day is a fresh opportunity to progress in my self-acceptance quest.

192. I am always embarking upon new paths of self-exploration and discovery.

193. I am a strong symbol of energy and vitality.

194. I am the one who knows the best way to meet my own requirements.

195. I release all resentment, even for myself.

196. I am caring and loving to both myself and all others that come into contact with me.

197. I end every day with loving acceptance of myself and all that I accomplished that day.

198. I do not dwell on my weaknesses, but I embrace my strengths.

199. Every day is a chance to grow and improve my relationship with myself.

200. I release all past regrets as an expression of the love that I have for myself in the present.

201. I embrace others with love, mercy, and forgiveness, just as I do for myself.

202. Because I love myself, I do not engage in self-sabotaging behavior.

203. Self-pity is a thing of the past.

204. My future is characterized by abundance and confidence.

205. I embrace and boldly declare all of my accomplishments with humility.

206. I am only constructive in my criticism for myself and others.

207. I provide feedback for others and myself with love.

208. I know how to make the very best decisions for me.

209. I have the courage to do what's best for me even if others are doing things differently.

210. I have empathy for my past pain and I work towards channeling it in a positive manner.

211. I am a very special gift to everyone around me.

212. The world is a better place because I am in it.

213. I make a positive impact on everyone I come in contact with.

214. I have total faith in myself at all times.

215. I can count on myself for anything I need.

216. I am dependable to myself and others.

217. I am becoming a much wiser person every single day.

218. My life serves as a great role model for others.

219. Other people are inspired by the way that I love myself.

220. I delight in my uniqueness and celebrate my differences.

221. I am completely worthy of success.

222. I am willing and able to change any part of myself that I believe needs improvement.

223. I have the power to adopt new skills.

224. I can forgive anyone because I have forgiven myself.

225. I am free to live in accordance with my highest self.

226. I choose to be happy because I deeply love myself.

227. Doing my best is all that I require of myself.

228. I never set expectations of myself out of fear.

229. I never set expectations of myself out of pain.

230. I never set expectations of myself out of low self-esteem or poor self-image.

231. I have a plan for my life and I love myself to follow through and execute it.

232. I have no reason to doubt what I can accomplish.

233. I have no reason not to believe in who I am.

234. I always find new reasons for me to keep loving myself.

235. I see myself as a person who succeeds in all areas of life.

236. A single failure does not diminish or negate my successes.

237. Falling short does not diminish my love for who I am.

238. I surrender doubt and worry.

239. Abundance is meant for me.

240. A prosperous life is ahead for me because I will attract with my love for myself.

241. I have the wisdom to know what I can handle at any given time.

242. I am patient with myself and do not demand of myself more than I can handle at any given time.

243. I am gentle and kind with myself when trying new things and exploring new territories.

244. I deeply trust myself in any situation that I encounter.

245. Where there is abundant self-love, there can be no fear or hatred.

246. Right here, just as I am, I am fully accepted.

247. Unconditionally loving myself is the best gift that I can give myself.

248. I do not require perfection in order to fully love myself for who I am.

249. My reach will always exceed my grasp because I will always pursue what I believe I am worthy of— even if it is difficult.

250. I love myself enough to break free from damaging addictions in all forms.

251. I give myself permission to thrive.

252. I have so many valuable gifts to give to the world.

253. I am amazed at what I have overcome to get to where I am today.

254. I am blessed to be in excellent health, and don't take that gift for granted.

255. I am open to receiving help when I need it in all types of relationships.

256. I release worries with calmness, love, and ease.

257. I know how to accept who I am and strive for who I want to be at the same time.

258. I can accomplish whatever it is that I choose to focus my energies and efforts on.

259. I love the feeling of self-love and acceptance.

260. I bring my best self to everything I do because I am worth it.

261. I bring my best into my relationships because I am worthy of having great relationships.

262. Because I love myself and my purpose, I am persistent in the fearless pursuit of my dreams.

263. I know that is normal to feel fear, and I persist forward regardless.

264. Loving myself means taking charge of my life and making it into the best it can possibly be.

265. My body has so much wisdom, and I choose to listen to it when it speaks.

266. I care for myself through daily practice of serenity and self-love.

267. Because I believe in myself, I can accomplish anything that I desire.

268. Everything in my world is well and good.

269. I know that loving myself means putting energy into what I am able to control.

270. I know that loving myself means graciously accepting what I cannot control.

271. I am totally grateful for all I have.

272. I am totally grateful for all I have done.

273. I am totally grateful for all I have become.

274. I wholly embrace changes with acceptance and peace.

275. I only accept circumstances that are worthy of me and my standards.

276. I choose to practice forgiveness to protect my own peace and sanity.

277. I choose to exercise patience to protect my own peace and sanity.

278. I have achieved success in every aspect of my life.

279. I am getting more and more wise through every experience.

280. I choose to protect my peace by living my life with a focused and calm energy.

281. I am gentle with myself as I work through my personal challenges.

282. I am full of love for who I am.

283. I express my ideas with clarity and confidence because I have a valuable perspective that people need to hear.

284. I am appreciative of my innate loving energy.

285. I am always evolving and making the most out of every chance to grow.

286. I welcome every imperfection that I have because I am in love with myself.

287. I have the emotional strength to show my true emotions without judging myself.

288. I am empowered and strong and in control of my life.

289. I do not allow myself to succumb to self-pity.

290. Self-discipline is one of the ways that I show myself true love.

291. I am disciplined in my actions because I believe in my future.

292. I take rest from my work when needed, knowing that my work does not determine my value.

293. Overworking myself is a form of compensating for what I may lack.

294. I have confidence in the goals I choose to pursue, and that is enough for me.

295. I am my biggest cheerleader and biggest fan.

296. I am resistant to the temptation of engaging in negative self-talk.

297. I love myself enough to always chase my dreams.

298. Because I love myself, I am able to better love others.

299. Although I am not what I do, I am proud of what I have done.

300. My self-love allows me to feel hope for my future.

301. I fully allow myself to love others to the degree to which I deserve love.

302. Intimacy with my loved ones flows from the strong love I have for myself.

303. I am completely safe in the comfort of my own body and mind.

304. If I ever feel stuck, I know that I can count on myself to get through it.

305. Everything is coming together for me.

306. I love my life.

307. I have a beautiful life that I am grateful to be living.

308. I am constantly putting in the work to become a better person.

309. I have the self-awareness to make improvements in myself where necessary.

310. Even while making self-improvements, I still love myself through the process.

311. I do not need to be hard on myself because I am capable of dealing with anything.

312. I am delighted in my presented circumstance.

313. I love myself enough to strive to become the best I can be.

314. I am not mentally burdened by any obstacles I may face.

315. I am loved despite what I perceive as my imperfections.

316. I am perfect in my imperfection.

317. What I consider flaws others consider as unique reasons to love me.

318. I am a very optimistic person, filled with life and joy.

319. I will always be more than enough for any endeavor that I pursue.

320. I love myself enough to always focus on seeing the positive.

321. I own my personal power, and no one can take that away from me.

322. I appreciate and love myself for getting me this far in life.

323. I take time out for self-care because I am worth it.

324. I invest in opportunities to treat myself because I am worth it.

325. I look for ways to exercise self-love.

326. I show self-love by pushing forward for another day.

327. Without regard to my achievements or lack thereof, I am deserving of respect and affection.

328. I accept and love myself without any conditions.

329. I have nothing except admiration and admiration for myself.

330. I take good care of myself and am proud of my appearance.

331. My very best is more than enough.

332. My self-confidence is strong enough to eradicate self-doubt.

333. I love myself enough to strive to make my life the best it can possibly be.

334. I believe in myself enough to want to see that I achieve my fullest possible potential.

335. I believe in myself and want to live my greatest life possible.

336. I love myself enough to create my dream life.

337. I easily and courageously step into my destiny.

338. All is moving towards things working out in my life.

339. I consciously choose to replace any negative ideas with good ones.

340. Even though I may not be there yet, I am on track to a greater future.

341. I'm putting forth the effort to become the most complete version of myself that I possibly can be.

342. I look within myself for peace and love.

343. What I do is meaningful and fulfilling.

344. Each of my days starts and ends in exactly the same manner: with an attitude of gratitude.

345. I constantly become mentally healthier by planting positive thoughts in my strong mind.

346. I am now loving myself more than I ever have, and that love will only continue to grow.

347. I let go of all unnecessary drama in my life because my peace is valuable to me.

348. I love the way my life has gone so far because it will lead me towards my best self.

349. I have a right to be healthy, loving and self-confident.

350. The most valuable love I can have is the love for myself.

351. I treat myself the way I expect others to treat me, and that is with love and respect.

Chapter 16
Affirmations for Accepting Yourself

Perhaps you might learn to embrace and respect your history as well as your present, so that negative ideas will no longer have the capacity to do you harm. Stop rejecting yourself for the way you looked or acted in the past. Learn to truly embrace the fact that the external world doesn't add to or take away the worthiness of your core being. You only acted the way you did because of your level of experience at the time. Stop beating up yourself over what you cannot change.

Accept that you are not perfect. It is your desire to be perfect that makes you conscious of yourself, worrying about what others are thinking of you.

The critic is very good at replaying scenes from your past that you find painful or embarrassing. It never forgets the names of people that hurt you in the past or occasions when you did something that made you feel like sinking into the ground with shame. When the critic attacks you with thoughts like this, simply observing and ignoring those thoughts can be very difficult.

Even though you see a beautiful face when you look into the mirror now, walking down the streets, thoughts of the times when you were too thin, pimple-faced and flat-chested cloud your mind. If you were taunted for the way you look, that is all you hear when you meet other people. It can be really hard to challenge or ignore your thoughts because the derogative words are so loud in your mind and the pictures are so clear—they were once your reality for a very long time.

The next crucial step you should practice after acceptance is forgiveness. Learning to love yourself regardless of what you think about yourself or your past memories. You will not be able to move on from the past if you continue to lament your acts and reject yourself.

Practicing the following "nevertheless: technique can help you make peace with your past. Select events or memories that are capable of eroding your self-esteem and respond with a 'nevertheless' statement. For instance, when your inner critic tells you that you can never amount to much, respond with, "I am not perfect, nevertheless I am growing."

Take your self-esteem assignment notebook and write on a fresh sheet, a list of three or more events or memories that always bring you down as you find them embarrassing and hurtful. Fully describe each of the memories or events and the emotional effect they had on you. Then create a perfect "nevertheless" response to each of those statements.

The Affirmations

1. I celebrate my individuality, no matter how others receive it.
2. I speak and think very highly of myself, and my actions reflect that.
3. I am worthy of success and happiness, so I work to achieve both.
4. Even though I strive to enhance myself, I am happy with who I am now.
5. I deserve and accept only the best.
6. I refuse to let anyone else's negative view of me hold me back.
7. I am worth investing time, money, an energy into my happiness and well-being.
8. I am in love with caring for my body, mind, and spirit.
9. I refuse to talk down to myself; I am amazing.
10. I acknowledge my self-worth on a daily basis.

11. I honor my commitments to myself.

12. I am proud of my roots and where I have come from.

13. I am proud of every mistake and misstep from my past, as it's led to who I am today.

14. I am a priority in my life, and I am treating myself as such.

15. I have faith in the kind of person I endeavor to become.

16. I am bursting with courage, strength, compassion, and love; I am enough.

17. I am loveable and worthy of greatness.

18. The only person or thing that can prevent me from living my greatest life is myself.

19. I make myself more and more proud every day.

20. I choose to be aligned with thoughts that heal my past.

21. I am letting go of others' expectations of me to attain my true self.

22. I am a work of art, made of infinite energy and possibility.

23. I love myself wholly and unconditionally; I am enough.

24. I have the power to choose to love myself and others.

25. I choose to think and feel positively about myself.

26. I am radiant and full of potential.

27. I serve as a positive example to others on how to love yourself.

28. I do not need the approval of others to give me permission to live my life.

29. I do not allow other people to get in the way of my self-confidence.

30. It is okay for me to love myself and simultaneously work to improve myself.

31. It is my mission to live my truth while motivating others to do the same.

32. I choose to build a positive image of myself for myself.

33. I am more than my body, and my body is more than its shape and size.

34. I decide how I feel and think, not only about myself, but everything.

35. I honor myself and the decisions I have made; I choose to be happy.

36. I find it easy to love myself.

37. I am giving it my all, and that is sufficient; I am sufficient.

38. I feel safe and confident in the way that I express myself.

39. I am divine, connected, and loved.

40. There is no wrong decision if I speak my truth.

41. It is always okay for me to be myself.

42. I am unique, and that is beautiful.

43. I do not compare myself and my success to others; everyone has a different path.

44. I respect myself and others with word, thought, and deed.

45. Everyone on the planet is different from me, and there is no one else quite like me.

46. I love myself, so I talk to myself like I would talk to someone I love.

47. My flaws do not define me or limit my worth.

48. The things about myself that I find imperfect, others find endearing.

49. I am a wonderful person from the inside out.

50. I allow myself to be myself, regardless of people accepting it.

51. I am committed to finding and fulfilling my purpose in life.

52. I am allowed to enjoy the abundance I deserve.

53. It is my differences that make me wonderful.

54. I am not perfect, and that is perfectly fine.

55. I do not need the approval of others in order to express my creativity.

56. I don't need approval from others in order to feel good about myself.

57. I am confident and proud of my achievements, past and future.

58. Imperfection is what makes me interesting.

59. Imperfection is what gives me reason to grow.

60. I honor my own goals, dreams, and desires.

61. I am uniquely talented, no matter what anyone else believes.

62. I have faith in my own abilities and my potential to achieve.

63. Today, I will love myself and all my flaws.

64. I wholly appreciate who I am and who I am striving to be.

65. My flaws do not make me any less love-able or less worthy of success.

66. I am radiating endless love towards myself and the world.

67. I forgive myself for all of the instances in the past that I haven't shown myself affection.

68. I show others the example of how to love me.

69. I show others the example of how to honor me.

70. I show others the example of how to respect me.

71. I show others the example of how to accept me.

72. I am accountable for my bad choices, but I forgive myself for them.

73. I now eliminate all self-doubt and forgive myself for harboring it in the past.

74. I forgive and accept all of my regrets, mistakes, and failures.

75. I do not sabotage myself with self-pity.

76. I pridefully embrace my accomplishments, results, and work.

77. No one has permission to hurt me, not even myself.

78. No one can make me feel less than, not even myself.

79. I do not need another person to complete me. I am already whole.

80. I find it easy to be myself.

81. I will love myself first so that I can spread love to others.

82. I love myself, what I have become, and who I can still be.

83. I determine my priorities for myself.

84. I recover from mistakes with grace.

85. I show mercy on myself for my missteps.

86. I am becoming wiser each day.

87. I am secure in my value.

88. I delight in sharing the gift of my uniqueness with the world.

89. I express myself freely, in ways that do not harm others.

90. I trade self-hatred for self-love.

91. I trade judgment for understanding.

92. I trust my actions and have faith in my decisions.

93. I practice having a pure perception of myself and others.

94. It is okay for me to change because that means I'm growing.

95. Being kind to myself is the first step to harmony and peace.

96. I am determined, confident, and courageous.

97. I deserve to be treated respectfully by myself and others.

98. I will stop being so hard on myself.

99. I am gentle and forgiving of my mistakes.

100. I am allowed to enjoy the things I have worked hard for.

101. I have total and absolute confidence in my own abilities.

102. Whether people praise me or speak ill of me, it does not affect my happiness.

103. Satisfaction and happiness come from within myself.

104. The only person I compare myself to is who I used to be.

105. It is quite OK for me to not know everything.

106. I respect myself and honor my values.

107. I do what I need to protect my content state of mind.

108. I give myself permission to make my own decisions.

109. All good things start with my ability to love myself first.

110. I admit my faults and allow myself to be corrected.

111. It is not necessary for me to be flawless to be lovable.

112. I tend to my emotional, mental, and spiritual needs.

113. I feel content, while I work to become my best self.

114. Self-acceptance can happen simultaneously with self-improvement.

115. Self-love can happen simultaneously with self-improvement.

116. Self-respect can happen simultaneously with self-improvement.

117. I express myself without inhibition.

118. I speak my mind without inhibition.

119. I treat myself with empathy, respect, and compassion.

120. It is up to me to choose what I believe and experience in my life.

121. I am in control of how I treat myself.

122. With each breath, I appreciate and cherish myself.

123. I do not hold past mistakes over my head.

124. I am worthy of having a peaceful mind.

125. I am proud of myself and all that I have accomplished so far in my life.

126. My self-image is in my own control.

127. I refuse to let other people's opinions of me lessen my self-worth.

128. My imperfections do not make me less worthy consideration from others.

129. I refuse to see myself as inferior; I am worthy of respect.

130. I am allowed to choose myself.

131. I am allowed to put myself first.

132. I can count on myself.

133. I reframe all my self-talk into positivity.

134. I deserve the very best.

135. I do not lower my standards to make others happy or more comfortable.

136. I choose to accept myself, while still working toward my betterment.

137. I choose to make love a part of my story.

138. Others accept me because I accept myself.

139. Others love me because I love myself.

140. Others respect me because I respect myself.

141. I do not judge myself for my fear, but I will not let it stop me from succeeding.

142. I commend myself for the progress I have made up until now.

143. I am fair to myself and others while working towards my goals.

144. I am allowed to feel emotions and express them without harming others.

145. I forgive myself for the times I did not give myself the respect I deserved.

146. I forgive myself for how I chose to survive in the past.

147. I forgive myself for indulging in things that do not fulfill me.

148. I forgive myself for all of the instances in which I was unable to offer value to the lives of others.

149. I forgive myself for not extending forgiveness to myself earlier.

150. I am a person of amazing character.

151. I appreciate all the positive traits I possess.

152. Every day, I learn to appreciate and love myself more and more.

153. I am friendly, reliable, and kind.

154. I have discovered that my happiness is independent of other people's opinions.

155. I will not feel guilty when others do not approve of what I say or do.

156. It is more important to grow from admitting a mistake than it is to be right.

157. I respect and love myself unconditionally.

158. I allow myself permission to be human and to make mistakes in my life.

159. I feel worthy of the love and success I deserve.

160. I will work towards understanding and improving my shortcomings.

161. Being authentic attracts more abundance than being perfect.

162. The transformation of my mind will take time, and there is nothing wrong with that.

163. I discard all fears of not being perfect.

164. What I am, have, or do is enough.

165. I will not hide my imperfections or be ashamed of them.

166. It is not necessary to accomplish perfection to feel appreciated.

167. I act positively towards others so I can act positively towards myself.

168. My imperfections do not make me flawed—they make me human.

Chapter 17
Affirmations for Controlling Yourself and Your Surroundings

When one's consciousness is focused on the present moment, while calmly noticing and accepting one's emotions, thoughts, and body sensations (mindfulness), one can attain a state of mind called mindfulness.

It is exhausting constantly judging ourselves, judging others, and judging everything happening around us. It takes away from the enjoyment of our own lives, and the constant need for perfection nicks away at our self-esteem because we always inevitably find ourselves unable to live up to what is in reality an impossible standard.

Wouldn't it be great to just be grateful? To fully experience the magic in everyday moments? To love and accept yourself fully despite being on a personal growth journey? To not feel like time is whizzing by as you collapse under the weight of a constant barrage of worries and responsibilities and time commitments?

There are so many responsibilities pulling us in a million different ways such that it's really easy to lose sight of what thing truly matters and get caught up in living in the future, never taking a minute to really appreciate what is in front of our eyes. I's easy to get the impression that every person or circumstance we come across is to be held accountable.

Everything is not about "black" or "white" or "right" or "wrong," although in the world of comparison traps we live in, it's easy to feel this way. Can you find value in the right now? Can what is ever be enough? It's going to have to be if you are ever going to be happy.

Accepting the way things are is not to be confused with settling or giving up all effort to attain growth and advancement. There is nothing wrong with becoming the best you possibly can be. In fact, you should. But acceptance is the place from which you can create the right emotional state to get there and become your highest self and live your greatest life.

So how do we cultivate acceptance? Sometimes a mental reset is just what we need to remind ourselves to slow down, stop judging ourselves, everyone, and everything so harshly, and be grateful. This produces just the mental clarity needed to get back to a mentally, emotionally, and spiritually healthy position from which life can actually be both enjoyed and advanced.

The use of affirmations is a highly efficient method of doing this. Affirmations can quite literally rewire your mind, by physically affecting the neural pathways in your brain. Affirmations, when spoken coupled with the feeling one would feel if they honestly believed them to be true, can be extremely powerful tools in improving and changing your life.

The Affirmations

1. I decide how I feel today.

2. My thoughts have the power to affect my reality, so I choose my thoughts wisely.

3. The most powerful tool I have is my freedom of choice.

4. I only put energy into positive thoughts that benefit my progress.

5. I am able to create a life full of happiness and abundance, and I choose to do so for myself.

6. I do not sweat the small things.

7. I take right actions and make right decisions for myself.

8. I do not allow my emotions to force me into impulsive decisions.

9. I attract the same energy that I put out into the world.

10. I will not stress over things I am unable to alter.

11. I can make the right decisions easily because I am clear on my priorities.

12. I choose to heal from the pains of my past.

13. I will exhaust all avenues in the pursuit of my goals.

14. I make my own happiness a priority.

15. I am not responsible for other people's beliefs, actions, or mistakes.

16. I make the deliberate choice to welcome new opportunities in my life.

17. I have infinite strategies to make my dreams come true.

18. I take responsibility for my life; I am the only one in charge of how my life turns out.

19. I choose to be motivated every day.

20. I turn my thoughts and ideas into action every day.

21. I am in control of my future, and I will continue to focus on the positive aspects of my life.

22. I choose to drop all excuses and make choices that contribute to my betterment.

23. It is okay for me to put myself first sometimes.

24. I thrive in adversity, which strengthens my character.

25. Every day, I am able to connect with myself on a deeper way.

26. I choose to be aligned with thoughts that promote a positive future.

27. I am always working to be my best self.

28. My strength is more powerful than any struggle.

29. I remove myself from any toxic environment that does not serve me.

30. I focus on achieving peace for myself.

31. I am at harmony with my environment.

32. I am not responsible for the responsibilities of others.

33. I speak up for my desires and ask for what I need.

34. I can guide myself in the correct direction.

35. I am always working on the improvement of my attitude.

36. I love myself enough to stick to the boundaries I have set.

37. I make choices that lead to happiness and joy.

38. Good things come to me from unexpected places.

39. I do not need to be saved. I am my own superhero.

40. I can say no with no problem, and I think for myself.

41. Giving in to self-doubt is not an option.

42. I walk away from any relationship that does not contribute to my well-being.

43. Where I feel weak, I hone resilience.

44. Only I can control my actions, reactions, and responses.

45. I refuse to let others make me forget what I deserve from life.

46. I practice self-discipline and self-awareness to attain my highest self.

47. My success, prosperity, and abundance are inevitable.

48. I am relentless, I persevere, and I keep going.

49. I am mentally strong and emotionally fit.

50. I refuse to wait for anyone else to make my dreams a reality.

51. I free myself of all bitterness and anger from the past, so I can be more receptive to the positive possibilities of the future.

52. I love myself enough to set and stick to boundaries.

53. I am allowed to change the direction of my life without anyone else's approval or validation.

54. I take responsibility for my mistakes.

55. I choose not to be afraid, but if I am, I move forward anyway.

56. I am allowed to say no to things that aren't best for me without feeling guilty.

57. I have infinite choices because opportunities are everywhere.

58. I am a powerful person, and I can change anything in my life that does not work for my greater good.

59. I acknowledge thoughts that do not serve me and let them go.

60. I do not make time for those who do not support my highest self.

61. I have the ability to exert control over my thoughts if I so choose.

62. I do not owe anyone an explanation for my choices.

63. I release my fears of imperfection because I am enough.

64. I have complete command of my thoughts and emotions.

65. I overcome my fears by taking action in the direction I want to go.

66. I abandon other people's expectations of me, freeing myself to live the life I want.

67. I create the life I desire.

68. I manage and control how I spend my time according to my priorities.

69. I do not compare myself to others.

70. I surrender my need to control others.

71. I control situations easily, with grace and confidence.

72. I cast away all things that do not help my personal or spiritual growth.

73. I do not waste my time being angry—I choose the peace of letting go.

74. I plan my work and follow through on my plans.

75. I choose freedom, liberating myself from things that block an open path.

76. Only I can control my life and govern my decision-making.

77. The judgments of others does not dictate my choices.

78. I move through my day with confidence.

79. I choose to heal my own life, taking responsibility for what I have done and for what I have allowed others to do to me.

80. I am independent, reliable, and capable of determining my own success.

81. In this moment, I take my power back.

82. I am balanced, connected, and at peace with myself.

83. I choose to be calm in my mind.

84. I commit only to things that support my dreams.

85. I acknowledge fear, but I do not give it the power to control me.

86. I am powerful and capable of anything.

87. I only project what I want out of life—infinite positivity.

88. I control my reactions; situations do not dictate how I respond.

89. I do all things with good intent and purpose.

90. I am not afraid of not knowing, because I am capable of learning.

91. I am capable of choosing how I feel about the things around me, and I always choose happiness and gratitude.

92. I make all decisions with confidence.

93. I will not settle for "good enough" when I know I am capable of greater.

94. If it is not true, I will not say it; if it is not right, I will not do it.

95. I focus my energy on building new things instead of lamenting over the demise of old things.

96. I will not let my emotions overpower my mental strength and intelligence.

97. I only accept positive vibes.

98. If I fear the unknown, I continue anyway. I let nothing stop me.

99. I do not seek revenge on anyone who has wronged me; I am at peace.

100. I create my own future and stand behind what I say and do with confidence.

101. I was not born to give up; I will persevere.

102. Fear is just an emotion; I forbid it to diminish my power.

103. I am letting go so that I can grow.

104. I will not let regret over my past keep me from the success of my future.

105. All that I do today will lead to a better tomorrow.

106. I trust and believe that what I seek is also seeking me.

107. I am in control of my actions and my reactions.

108. I do not hold anyone else responsible for my own happiness.

109. My discipline gives way to happiness.

110. I deal with stressful situations calmly.

111. I reject all habits, actions, and people that do not empower me.

112. The power to realize my dreams is within me.

113. I accept my situation so that I can change it.

114. I am naturally calm, cool, and collected.

115. Today, I will strive to make positive changes.

116. I am able to acknowledge my emotions without letting them control me.

117. I am powerful enough to determine my own future, regardless of other people's opinions.

118. I deal with challenging emotions in a positive and productive way.

119. I think logically and clearly, even in high pressure situations.

120. I have no control over the acts of other people, but I do have control over my own actions.

121. Sometimes, I need to relinquish control, and that's alright.

122. I will accomplish great things, and nothing can stand in my way.

123. My happiness relies not on who I am or what I have, but what I think.

124. Each and every day, I am choosing, not waiting to be chosen.

125. I have control over my thoughts; I have control over my life.

126. I live my life impressing myself, not others.

127. I have all the energy and time I need to accomplish my goals because I create it.

128. I am shaped by my thoughts. I become what I think. So I choose my thoughts wisely.

129. I do not make decisions just to impress others.

130. Moderating and managing my emotions comes naturally to me.

131. I may bend, but I do not ever break.

132. I am the source of my inner peace in the midst of outside chaos.

133. I trust my inner voice and its ability to show me the way.

134. I stick to my values, no matter what other people think.

135. I extract the lesson out of every apparent loss.

136. I can save myself; I do not need to be saved.

137. My efforts have value, even if the outcome is unexpected.

138. I work to understand those who have done me wrong, so I can forgive them and protect my personal peace.

139. Success will come to me through my courage and determination.

140. I make a choice, daily, to radiate positivity and optimism.

141. I do not alter my ideas for the sake of fitting other people's opinions.

142. No one else can achieve success for me; it is my responsibility.

143. Nothing will make me satisfied unless I choose to be happy.

144. I stay true to my personal decisions and life choices.

145. I make my own decisions, undeterred by the opinions of others.

146. I stand by my decisions with confidence and pride.

147. I reap the benefits from being in control of my emotions.

148. I have the ability to be better and will always strive to do so.

149. Those who are likewise on a personal development and improvement journey are the only people with whom I associate.

150. I recognize that individuals perceive the world in a variety of ways, but I stay committed to my own set of principles.

151. My happiness does not come to me; it comes from me.

152. It is my responsibility to solve my own problems.

153. I am intentional in what I do, hear, experience, and see.

154. I challenge my past bad decisions and learn from them.

155. I have a productive, enjoyable daily routine that breeds my success.

156. I do not allow others to take advantage of me, nor do I take advantage of others.

157. I do not always have to be right, but I am always gracious and kind.

158. I do not settle where I am if I know I can do far better.

159. I am disciplined and self-aware.

160. I choose to create a healthy environment for myself that fosters my growth and productivity.

161. I effortlessly embody humility and compassion.

162. I lead my life with self-awareness and self-correction.

163. I am my own source of validation.

164. I do not let the past control my present and future actions.

165. I accept that the past is unchangeable and resolve any anger or hurt associated with it.

166. I stand by my decisions with conviction.

167. I take consistent intentional action towards my dreams to ensure my success.

168. My personal peace is my priority.

169. I choose to manifest greatness in my life in this moment and the next.

170. Other people's needs are equally as essential as mine, and vice versa.

171. I cannot control other people's thoughts about me; I think of myself positively regardless.

172. Even though I face obstacles, I will persevere.

173. I choose not to make excuses, no matter what.

174. I love the feeling of working hard for my goals and seeing the rewards of my efforts.

175. If it is to be done, it is up to me.

176. I am up for the task of creating my best life.

177. I remain calm within no matter what is going on outside of me.

178. Self-control and self-discipline come easily to me.

179. I choose to make myself and others happy.

180. I choose to make forgiveness a part of my narrative.

181. I choose to be productive, taking consistent steps toward fulfilling my goals.

182. I am kind to others, and unbothered by outside opinions.

183. My dedication to my goals is unshakeable.

184. Peace is a natural, effortless part of who I am.

185. I am committed to reaching all of my objectives.

186. I choose to make happiness a part of my story.

187. I have chosen to concentrate on the things that are important to me in life.

188. My self-discipline helps me reach my goals.

189. I surround myself with individuals that are always striving to improve themselves.

190. I choose to fail forward, using every mistake as an opportunity to improve.

191. My self-discipline comes naturally.

192. Opportunities are everywhere, so I have unlimited choices.

193. I have an abundant amount of willpower.

194. I cultivate habits that help me achieve my goals and dreams.

195. I choose to see the lessons in my mistakes.

196. No one can do for me what I won't do for myself.

197. I make gratitude and joy my emotional habits.

198. Today, I choose to take one step further than I did yesterday.

199. I do not live by chance. I live by choice.

200. I have made the decision to accept responsibility for my actions.

201. No matter how high the mountain is, I will climb it.

202. I attract things and people that encourage my growth.

203. Being positive is a choice I commit to every day.

204. I always keep my calm and stay in control of my emotions so I can stay in control of myself.

205. I can and I will, and that's all there is to it.

206. I train my body, feed my spirit, and focus my mind.

207. The past, present, and future will not be changed by my overthinking.

208. I acknowledge guilt as a feeling and not a fact.

209. I believe in what I want so much that it has no choice but to materialize.

210. I choose to get rid of my old habits that do not serve my goals.

211. I accept full responsibility for the decisions I have made.

212. I separate myself from unhelpful obsessive thoughts.

213. I choose to be a priority in my life.

214. What I am is the result of how I think of myself, so my thoughts will be positive.

215. I am responsible for the energy that I release into the world, so I will only emanate positivity.

216. Today, I am focused on my goals, and I will do what I can to achieve them.

217. I can change my life and experience whenever I want.

218. I choose not to give my power to anyone else.

219. My body is a representation of everything I put into it, physically and mentally.

220. I choose to be in a positive environment where I can be my best self.

221. I always have a choice; it is up to me to make the best one.

222. I feel empowered by taking inspired action.

223. Today, I choose presence over regret.

224. I have the strength and willpower to work around any challenges I may face.

225. I cannot control the world, but I can control how I respond to challenges against peace.

226. I alone am in full control of how I choose to live my life.

227. I have the power to choose success and prosperity.

Chapter 18
Affirmations for Relationships and Supporting Others

Ever been around people who walk into a room and instantly brighten it with their presence, drawing people to them and making them feel welcome for reasons they can't quite put their finger on? Have you ever been in a place when someone comes in and the tone quickly dips and shifts in a manner that is both physical and difficult to articulate? Isn't it interesting how some individuals appear to be happy all of the time, no matter what is going on around them? Do you actually know someone who is always in a state of crisis, where something is always going wrong or falling apart in their life, and where everyone and everything seems to be conspiring against them? Do you know someone like this?

For those of you who actually have had the opportunity to tour the globe, you are well aware that a number of the world's most poor people, living in the most difficult of conditions, are blissfully happy. Yet, close to home, you might witness wealthy individuals who seem to have it everything, yet are terribly unhappy. Happiness has nothing to do with what occurs outside of yourself. It all comes down to what is going on inside of you.

It is your frame of mind that makes all the difference. Disempowering ideas may make you feel powerless and hopeless, and they can be difficult to overcome. And since these negative beliefs are often anchored in our subconscious, we are often unaware of the psychological harm we cause ourselves. In contrast, instructing your brain to be cheerful and optimistic while anticipating favorable outcomes for yourself and others may make the difference between experiencing success and experiencing failure.

A successful life is a happy life, and vice versa. And a happy life is a successful life—whatever way you choose to define success is up to you. But it all just really starts (and ends) with the mind, with molding and training it to think in the manner in which you choose.

The use of affirmations is a highly efficient method of doing this. Affirmations have the ability to essentially rewire your brain by physically altering the neuronal connections in your brain, according to research. As long as they are stated in conjunction with the emotion one would have if one really thought what they are saying to be true, affirmations may be incredibly effective tools for improving and transforming one's life.

The habit of pleasant thoughts and a cheerful temperament will make it simple for you to be happy whatever or no matter what your circumstances, and it will be easy for you to bounce back from times of difficulty if you cultivate these habits. You'll also notice that the happier you get, the more that positive events will occur in your life. Moreover, without cultivating a habit of happiness and optimism, you will discover that happiness will constantly evade you no matter how favorable your life circumstances seem to be at any one point in time. Furthermore, the more negatively you see the world around you, the worse things will become for you.

Life is a gift that should be loved and enjoyed every day; instead, the majority of people walk through existence merely waiting for the day to finish, as if life itself is a weight to be carried. Happiness does not come easy to everyone in every situation. Happiness is a learned behavior. Happiness is something that may be chosen. What happens to us is not always under our control, but we have the ability to select our behavior in response to what occurs. Furthermore, optimism and pleasure are always preferable to pessimism and sorrow.

Get your mental peace back, your pleasure back, and the great things you want to bring into your life by doing so. Get the rock solid foundation in place now so that you may look at life with a half-full perspective in the future.

The Affirmations

1. I foster supportive, loving relationships which increase my long-term happiness.

2. My optimistic attitude allows me to build good relationships and strong friendships.

3. I attract healthy and happy personal relationships by projecting a positive attitude.

4. I make others around me happier through my positive attitude.

5. I use empathy and sympathy to support others in their times of need.

6. My positive outlook contributes to my success in my relationships and my overall life.

7. I have an infectious laugh and smile that improves the moods of people around me.

8. I have a network of successful, inspiring people who motivate me to succeed.

9. My friends and I push each other to become the best versions of ourselves.

10. When I need them, my buddies are always there for me, no matter what.

11. I always make room for quality time with my loved ones.

12. I am in relationships that are emotionally supportive and fulfilling.

13. My relationships both comfort me and challenge me.

14. I have mentors and models in every area of my life who inspire me to become better.

15. My significant other and I bring out the best in each other.

16. I possess willpower and self-control, which positively benefits my romantic and social relationships.

17. I surprise strangers and the people in my life with random acts of kindness to brighten their day.

18. I encourage my family and friends to do well because I want to see them at their best.

19. I am respectful of viewpoints and opinions that are different from my own.

20. My agreeable and happy disposition strengthen my connections with others.

21. I grow more and more empathetic every day.

22. My positive outlook attracts positive friends and contributes to further happiness.

23. I am fortunate to have close personal and professional relationships that make me happy.

24. I openly share my thoughts and feelings with my loved ones.

25. My openness with my feelings relieves stress and makes me feel stronger emotionally.

26. I am able to remain positive and optimistic no matter who I am around.

27. I am encouraging to others when they are in need of a mood boost.

28. I am easily able to be patient with my friends, family, and partner.

29. The patience I possess strengthens the emotional bonds in my relationships.

30. My positive attitude is contagious to all who come in contact with me.

31. I support my significant other, friends and family whenever I can because it makes them happy to know I care.

32. I treat people in the same manner in which I would want to be treated.

33. I am happier when I have stronger social connections and familial bonds.

34. My positive relationships with friends and family positively contribute to my self-confidence.

35. I value the quality of my relationships with my partner, friends, and family.

36. I provide support and unconditional love to myself and to those around me.

37. All of my relationships with friends, family, and loved ones are built on trust, honesty, and loyalty.

38. I make an effort to create and nourish positive relationships and get to know people better.

39. My close relationships contribute to increased happiness for both me and the other people involved.

40. I radiate and project positive energy, which attracts high quality people and relationships to me.

41. I relish the moments that I spend with my partner, friends, and family.

42. I put effort into creating opportunities to strengthen the bonds between me and the people I love.

43. I love laughing with my loved ones because it is good for my mental and physical health.

44. I am there for my social and personal connections when they need me.

45. I make an effort to do things for my partner, friends, and family that make them happy.

46. My passion and positivity inspire others around me to feel joy and happiness.

47. I happily celebrate and recognize the successes of my peers.

48. I make myself available to talk to and emotionally support my loved ones whenever they need me.

49. I build trust in my personal and work relationships by delivering on my promises.

50. I freely give compliments to others to improve their happiness, outlook and self-esteem.

51. I form and nurture relationships by creating and participating in social events regularly.

52. I interact more with people who matter most in my life, than I do with screens and electronic devices.

53. I voluntarily reach out to others and offer help even if they have not asked me for it.

54. When it comes to others' happiness, I make an effort to be aware of their needs.

55. I expand other people's networks by bringing people together.

56. I create opportunities for me and my loved ones to enjoy doing things together that we love.

57. I work well with others in professional environments.

58. I have strong connections with the people I work with.

59. I make an effort to regularly call the people I love and remind them that I care.

60. I always find thoughtful ways to show my significant other that I care.

61. I share things that make me happy with other people so it can also make them happy and brighten their day.

62. I make an attempt to meet new individuals who have interests in common with me.

63. My time is my most valuable asset, and I show others that I love them when I choose to spend it with them.

64. I use my talents and ideas to help others.

65. I strengthen my relationships when I share my gifts with others, rather than keep them to myself.

66. I sometimes make healthy sacrifices for the people close to me in order to make them happy.

67. I make an effort to dedicate time to talking and listening to my partner, friends, and family.

68. I make myself emotionally available to my loved ones.

69. I openly express gratitude to my loved ones to thank them for all they've done for me.

70. Whenever I am with a loved one, I am fully physically, mentally, and emotionally present.

71. I constantly look for and discover ways to connect with people over similar interests.

72. I look for ways to help others to decrease their stress and lessen their burdens.

73. I look for ways to help make other people happier.

74. I acknowledge the importance of communication in any successful relationship.

75. My communication abilities are continuously being refined, and I am continually striving for improvement.

76. I spontaneously plan fun, shared experiences with my loved ones to bring us closer.

77. I am there for my loved ones in times of sickness and in health.

78. I am a reliable source of positive energy to others in their darkest times of need.

79. I let my loved ones know I care through my actions as well as my words.

80. I take joy in creating opportunities to bring others joy.

81. No matter how busy I get, I always set aside time for the people I love.

82. When it comes to my spouse, friends, and family, I make an effort to be attentive to their needs.

83. My life is more fulfilling because of my wonderful relationships.

84. I am positive and encouraging to everyone, which makes people love being around me.

85. I offer positive and constructive feedback to people without being negative or overly critical.

86. I amplify my enjoyment of the things I love by sharing them with the people I love.

87. I do good things for others without being asked.

88. I am a strong, positive influence on others, and I help people cultivate a positive mindset.

89. I make an effort to provide emotional support for others when they are not at their best.

90. I am fun to be around because I am happy.

91. I make an effort not to isolate myself because being around others brings me joy.

92. I am a ray of sunshine, who brightens other's people's days when they are feeling down.

93. I find that I am happier in my romantic relationships because of my optimism.

94. I am able to provide emotional support for other people and still maintain my positivity and optimism at the same time.

95. I find and share positive solutions to other people's problems with ease.

96. I realize that everyone has the right to express their own point of view.

97. It is easy for me to constantly meet new people and cultivate new friendships.

98. I enjoy meeting people from different backgrounds because it makes me more empathetic and open minded.

99. I believe in my partner, friends, and family and I motivate them to do and achieve their best.

100. My effortlessly social nature and positive attitude make it easy to meet people for romantic relationships.

101. My effortlessly social nature and positive attitude make it easy to meet people for platonic relationships.

102. I realize that everyone has the right to express their own point of view.

103. I accept people who think and believe differently than I do.

104. I respect the privacy and personal time for both me and the people I am in relationships with.

105. I keep an open mind and avoid being judgmental of others.

106. I know that good relationships take work and I am willing and able to happily put the work in.

107. My positive attitude provides strength and longevity for my relationships.

108. I take good care of myself, which helps me more easily attract good romantic and platonic relationships.

109. I always find time and ways to send positive messages to the people I love and care about.

110. I accept my loved ones for who they are and respect opinions that differ from my own.

111. I accept my loved ones for who they are and respect their choices that differ from my own.

112. I choose to only spend time in my life with supportive, positive, and uplifting people.

113. I make an effort to fully show up in my life and relationships.

114. I accept myself, which allows me to accept others.

115. I have a strong professional network that supports and contributes to my career success.

116. I make an effort to make gestures, big and small, to show love for my loved ones.

117. I have a romantic partner who fully supports and loves me, and I do the same for them.

118. I sometimes put my own desires aside and do things I don't want to do because I know it is important to a person I love.

119. I am always honest because trust is the foundation of my personal relationships.

Chapter 19
Affirmations for Taking Accountability and Responsibility

Now that you are aware of your core values, it is time to reframe the way you see your mistakes. No matter how conscious you are of your primary principles, you will make mistakes from time to time. However, mistakes on their own have no power to upset your mental balance or water down the progress you've made so far in building a healthy self-esteem; it is your rationalization of these mistakes that has a devastating effects on it.

Trying to live your life by the high, incomprehensible or unrealistic standards of your parents or society is one reason why you feel the way you do about mistakes. If you've always heard that you should not spend money on different personal products as they are vanity. You will find yourself feeling bad and regretting the few times you went against that rule and trying your best to avoid making such a "mistake" again.

You believe your critic when it tells you that the mistakes you've made are proof of how worthless you are. But the truth is, mistakes are inevitable, and you can't be perfect at all times—which is okay. You need to consciously work on how you view mistakes.

The best way to handle mistakes is to start seeing them as:

1. **A learning process:** stop ruminating on previous errors and berating yourself for them, reminding yourself that you should just have done things differently in the future. You've learned your lesson and are less likely to make the same mistake again. If you had known what you know now, you probably wouldn't have behaved in such a reckless manner in the first place. Don't stop yourself from being spontaneous or trying new things

because you fear failing or making a mistake. Your mindset should be: "if I get it wrong, I'll at least learn the right way to do it next time."

2. **A natural part of your life:** No one in life is perfect, which is natural. Feel free to express your thoughts and do what you want. If your words or actions disappoint someone or make you feel awkward, remember that you cannot always be perfect – you can either learn from the mistakes or move on.

The Affirmations

1. I am here today as a result of the actions I took yesterday.
2. If I don't like something in my life, I will change it.
3. Things only change when my actions change.
4. Things only change when my attitude changes.
5. I am responsible for all results that happen as a result of my actions.
6. I am in control of my thoughts and I choose to think positively.
7. I take the steps necessary to ensure that I am mentally free and clear enough to achieve achievement.
8. I take a step each day to grow wealth tomorrow.
9. The problems in my life are my fault and not the fault of others.
10. There is no such thing as luck, I create my own fortune.
11. My financial success depends on my own actions, not on the economy.

12. My financial success depends on my own actions, not on the political climate.

13. My financial success depends on my own actions, not my upbringing.

14. My financial success depends on my own actions, not others around me.

15. I control my own financial future and I choose prosperity.

16. I create my own reality with my own thoughts.

17. I can change the circumstances around me with right thought and action.

18. I believe I can, I am certain that I can, and I will.

19. I have complete control over my destiny.

20. I will do whatever it takes within moral and ethical reason to succeed.

21. When I do something wrong, I take action to make it right.

22. Talk is cheap; I grow my success by action and results.

23. I accept each new challenge as an opportunity for growth.

24. I take responsibility for who I am today.

25. I accept that I have created the bad as well as the good in my life.

26. If I don't like the way my life is going, it is my responsibility to do something about it.

27. I am responsible for changing my own life; nobody else can do it for me.

28. Takers lose and givers win. I choose to be a giver.

29. It is my own actions that decide my level of success in every aspect of my life.

30. When I provide value to others, I receive money and financial success in return.

31. I am responsible for how I perceive adversity.

32. I am responsible for how I respond to adversity.

33. I am in control of my reactions to situations around me.

34. I am in control of my habits and impulses.

35. I have the ability to create good new habits and get rid of bad old ones.

36. I am in control of my mood and temper and always find a positive way to react to any situation.

37. I alone am responsible for my happiness.

38. I am responsible for my career situation and will change it if I don't like it.

39. I accept that everything I did before has lead me to the point where I am today.

40. For better or worse, I am the sum total of all of my choices.

41. If I want my life to be better, I have to make better decisions.

42. My own health is in my control.

43. I accept responsibility for any failures in my life.

44. I learn from each apparent failure in my life.

45. I choose to reframe what seems like failure as a lesson I will use to succeed next time.

46. I am responsible for the income I generate.

47. No matter the outcome of my life, I either created it or allowed it.

48. No matter my circumstances, I have the ability to turn my life around.

49. I am responsible for using my unique gifts and talents to the maximum extent possible.

50. I take responsibility to learn the skills and gain the education I need to achieve success.

51. I take responsibility for listening to others when they offer constructive criticism.

52. I am responsible for my current financial situation and will take specific actions to change it if I am not happy about it.

53. I am solely accountable for the words that come out of my lips, which have the potential to negatively affect my professional or commercial performance.

54. I am responsible for the quality of the thoughts in my head.

55. The problems I perceive in my life are all fixable.

56. I adopt a wealth mentality to ensure my financial success.

57. I am responsible for my past.

58. I am responsible for my present.

59. I am responsible for my future.

60. I want to do all in my ability to guarantee that my future is as bright as possible.

61. I have total power over how I react to whatever occurs in my life at any time.

62. I have the power to turn any negative into a positive.

63. I have the power to perceive any negative as a positive.

64. The life that I am leading is the life that I chose through my actions.

65. It is my responsibility to take action to correct any mistakes that I have made.

66. I take responsibility for seeing the good in other people.

67. I choose to speak kindly about others.

68. I take responsibility for the price I must pay for success.

69. If there is a better way to do something, I realize I must discover this for myself.

70. I own my mistakes and take action to correct them.

71. I accept responsibility for my physical health and recognize that I alone can change it.

72. I accept responsibility for the status of my relationships and recognize that I alone can change them.

73. I am responsible for my feelings.

74. I am in control of my emotions.

75. I take action to maintain mental strength and clarity.

76. I own my energy.

77. I am responsible for where I am in my life, not my friends.

78. I am responsible for where I am in my life, not my family.

79. I am responsible for where I am in my life, not my government.

80. I am responsible for where I am in my life, not my boss.

81. I point the finger at myself first, not others.

82. I always find a way to make it happen.

83. I make results, not excuses.

84. Nothing holds me back from achieving success.

85. No one holds me back from achieving success.

86. Every single day I take at least one step to become more responsible over my own life.

87. I choose my response in the face of a challenge.

88. I cannot control other people and how they perceive me, but I can put my best foot forward at all times.

89. I am responsible for always being prepared.

90. I am responsible for saving money for financial emergencies.

91. I am responsible for my own fate and do not depend on anyone else to keep my ship afloat.

92. I am responsible for the people I allow into my life.

93. No one is coming to save me, I have to better my own life if I want it to be better.

94. I take full responsibility for the person I become tomorrow as a result of the actions I am taking today.

95. I choose to better my surroundings with right thought and action.

96. I live a life of no excuses and no regrets.

97. I am not responsible for the circumstances I was born into, but I am responsible for every action I've taken since.

98. I always have a choice.

99. My past negative experiences have no bearing on my future success.

100. I am strong and in complete control of my own destiny.

101. I am a shot taker and a way maker.

102. I depend only on myself for my financial success.

103. Anything I want, I can create.

104. I confront challenges head on.

105. Past failures and struggles are a result of my attitude, which I take full responsibility for now.

106. Past failures and struggles are a result of my actions, which I take full responsibility for now.

107. I recognize that if my life isn't going right, I am the one who needs to change.

108. Whenever I don't like the way I feel, I change the behaviors that cause those feelings.

109. I choose to adopt a positive attitude each and every single day.

110. I embrace change as an opportunity for growth.

111. I always see the positive in everything that happens.

112. I always see the positive in every person I cross paths with.

113. The problems in my life are all temporary and easier to overcome than I think.

114. I am the only one who can change how I feel inside.

115. I do not compare myself to others.

116. I understand that I am running my own race.

117. I take responsibility for remaining humble and true to myself as my wealth increases.

118. I replace scattered thinking with specific goals to improve my life.

119. I refuse to engage in self-pity.

120. I do not manipulate others by trying to get them to feel pity for me.

121. When under pressure, I maintain my cool and composure.

122. I am flexible and resourceful when things don't go my way.

123. I am social and friendly and take initiative in social situations.

124. I have a healthy social life that helps keep my mind on positive things.

125. I fill each of my days with joy and laughter.

126. I replace thoughts of self-pity with concern for others.

127. I am responsible for providing the service to others that leads to my own wealth.

128. There is always money to be made, and I will not let external circumstances control my fate.

129. I replace impatience with persistence and hard work.

130. I am honest, and people are honest with me.

131. I take action to ensure that I am always full of energy and vitality.

132. I wake up each day feeling optimism, hope, and love.

133. I can and will change any situation that I don't like.

134. I am always open to change and embrace it.

135. I accept assistance from others when I am in need of it.

136. I seek answers when I don't already know them.

137. I am open to the idea that someone else may know more than me.

138. I am open to the idea that someone else may know better than me.

139. I am responsible for making every moment of every day fulfilling.

140. I move forward past fear when it arises.

141. I am confident and optimistic about my future.

142. I am passionate about my life, present and future.

143. I realize that every decision I've made up to this point has led me to where I am right now.

144. I keep my mind fixed on positive and uplifting things.

145. I guard my mind and only allow positive thoughts and images to enter it.

146. It can be done, and I can do it.

147. I don't let anything stop me from moving towards my goals.

148. What I see in my mind, I create in my life, so I take full responsibility for my life vision.

149. When I feel frustration, I calmly find a way forward.

150. When I need assistance or support, I seek it.

151. I offer help and support when I am able to.

152. I am reliable and dependable.

153. I keep my promises to others.

154. I take my commitments seriously.

155. I own my reputation and every part I played in creating it.

156. I am responsible for keeping my mind in a happy state.

157. What I perceive to be problems in my life can all be used to my advantage.

158. Anything that is wrong, I can make right.

159. There are no limitations to what I am capable of

160. I am a good steward of my finances.

161. I am responsible for responsible spending.

162. I always live within my financial means.

163. I am deliberate about filling my time with activities that push me forward.

164. I am deliberate about filling my time with activities that I enjoy.

165. I am intentional about spending my time with positive people that I love.

166. I alone control my attitude about money, success, and prosperity.

167. Instead of living on auto-pilot, I take direct control over my outcomes.

168. I choose to seek and find opportunities instead of obstacles.

169. I seek joy; therefore, I find joy.

170. I seek love; therefore, I find love.

171. I seek success; therefore, I find success.

172. For the sake of success, I am prepared to set my ego aside and do whatever it takes.

173. I am responsible for acting with maximum efficiency and efficacy.

174. It is up to me to improve my skills as needed.

175. My financial success is not controlled by big corporations or big government.

176. I am willing to pay the short-term price for long-term success.

177. I accept the consequences for all of my actions.

178. I am prepared to be the first to provide a helping hand if someone needs it.

179. I always pay it forward.

180. I make the first move, and don't wait for others to.

181. I am strong enough to overcome any and every obstacle I face with grace.

Chapter 20
Affirmations for Self-Confidence

The biggest contributor to success and happiness is the ability to be yourself - to boldly display your personality and make choices that are faithful to your own beliefs. It comes from making a positive difference in the world by using your particular talents. It's important to stand out and make your voice heard, even if what you're about to say will be controversial. Always remain true to yourself no matter what. These things are all indicative of the confidence that allows people to get ahead in their careers, enjoy amazing personal relationships, and acquire a high self-esteem and personal inner peace.

So many of us are afraid of making connections with others for fear of rejection, thinking that when people love us, we will love ourselves, and if people accept us, we will be confident—when it is the other way around. When we love ourselves, people will love us. And if we are confident, people will accept us. It all boils down to confidence.

We are all born with confidence, but over time, as we transition through adolescence and adulthood, rejections, difficulties, and cruel people of the world we encounter growing up whittle away at it, causing social anxiety, unhealthy self-criticism, and feelings of inadequacy. And while we go about our daily lives, we are frequently unaware of the negative ideas and sentiments that are ingrained in our subconscious, which further undermines our self-confidence, causing even further psychological damage to our psyches.

To regain your self-confidence and believe that you are sufficient, you must first believe in yourself by retraining and reprogramming your brain. The use of affirmations is a highly efficient method of doing this. Affirmations can quite literally rewire your mind, by physically affecting the neural pathways in your brain. Affirmations, when spoken coupled with the feeling one would feel if they honestly believed them to be true, can be extremely powerful tools in improving and changing your life.

If you would like to them as meditation, before you begin, find a quiet place where you will remain undisturbed for the entire length of the audio. Then, remove all distractions. Turn off your phone, eliminate as much noise as possible, close the door to where ever you are, and alert anyone around you not to disturb you for the next two hours. When you're ready to begin, find a comfortable position, either sitting up or laying down, and be sure to remove all physical tension from your body.

Choose a position comfortable enough for you to allow the muscles of your body to relax but that will also ensure you stay awake. Many people like to sit with their legs crossed and their hands resting palms up or down on their knees. Some people prefer to lay on their backs, with their palms up by their sides. Choose whichever is best for you.

Then, once you are settled into position, you can either choose a spot to look at and drop your eyelids and soften your gaze; or you can close your eyes altogether. Begin clearing your mind of all past, present, and future thoughts and worries and deepen your relaxed state by slowing your breathing to long breaths, fully inhaling then fully exhaling. When you feel you are adequately relaxed, let the words seep into your mind and your consciousness, or repeat them in your head at intervals.

It doesn't matter how you choose to meditate, as all of methods can be effective and make a noticeable difference in your state of mind and future success. With meditation through affirmations, you can not only consciously absorb these thoughts, but you can simultaneously subconsciously absorb them as well. The essential thing to remember is to maintain consistency. Whatever you do, make sure you do it every day—even multiple times a day if you have time.

You can begin your day with affirmations and end it with meditation and meditation. But just keep doing it. Change will not happen overnight. It will really take time to retrain your mind to think in a more productive manner, but I guarantee you that the work will be well worth it.

The Affirmations

1. I will never apologize for being my true self.
2. I am a strong and confident person.
3. I live my life unaffected by fear.
4. I live my life unaffected by doubt.
5. I can make it through anything.
6. Resilience and perseverance are part of who I am.
7. I have perfect health mentally, emotionally and physically.
8. No matter what happens, I can always make the best of it.
9. No matter what happens, I will always make the best of it.
10. I can have anything I want in this life.
11. I can do anything I want in this life.
12. I can become anything I want in this life.
13. My conscience is trustworthy, and I will lean on it for guidance and peace.
14. My views and opinions are all important and they have value to others and myself.
15. I speak up for what I believe in, regardless of what other people think.

16. I can become successful at anything I put my mind to.

17. I am unafraid to express my feelings.

18. I boldly express my thoughts.

19. All of my thoughts are rooted in self-confidence and love.

20. Where I am today is exactly where I am meant to be.

21. I only attract and allow amazing and loving people into my life.

22. I act as a magnet for wealth and success, attracting them to me.

23. I am worthy of all things that will lift me up and improve my life.

24. I attract love into my life by the power of the love I have for myself.

25. I own my weakness and mistakes with confidence and pride.

26. I know that everything will always work out for me in the end.

27. I possess wisdom, to the benefit of myself and others.

28. My inner self is not bound by the limitations of my physical body.

29. I deserve a bright and abundant future and it is coming my way.

30. I have the mental strength to handle all of life's challenges.

31. I live my life with certainty and confidence.

32. I have confidence in where I am and where I am going.

33. I am productive and efficient in all of my tasks that lead me towards my ultimate goals.

34. I have an abundance of talents that will serve to elevate my life in the best way possible.

35. I have an abundance of talents that will elevate the lives of others.

36. I am unapologetic about who I am.

37. I am unapologetic about what I can accomplish.

38. I have what it takes to achieve whatever I desire.

39. I will overcome any and all obstacles that try to stand in my way.

40. Success is just who I am.

41. Success is inevitable for me.

42. Nothing can ever keep me from achieving my dreams.

43. I am stronger than fear.

44. I am stronger than doubt.

45. Fear and doubt are not strong enough to discourage me from forging ahead.

46. I make the most of my talents and natural abilities.

47. I trust my internal wisdom to guide me towards prudent decisions.

48. I easily handle criticism and feedback with grace.

49. I love my talents no matter what others may think.

50. I am intelligent and attractive and this is how I am viewed by everyone.

51. I am fully comfortable in my own skin.

52. I believe in myself in a way that is palpable to others.

53. My skills and abilities will inevitably lead me to professional success.

54. I am respected and admired by others.

55. I do meaningful, important, and rewarding work.

56. I make significant contributions to the world in ways that only I can.

57. The work that I do with my natural talents positively impacts others around me.

58. I wholeheartedly believe in my ability to make a positive impact through my work.

59. I am capable of creating intelligent and effective plans for my future.

60. I attract wealth and prosperity in abundance.

61. The future is in my hands.

62. I pursue my deepest desires regardless of any resistance that may arise.

63. I love myself and every part of me, and others do too.

64. I am never a victim, and I always take control and responsibility over my life.

65. I can turn around any situation or circumstance for the better.

66. My circumstances are subject to the amount of faith and effort I put in to change them.

67. I easily find new ways of thinking and solving problems.

68. I am only in competition with myself.

69. I never give up on myself, no matter what.

70. I am more than good enough.

71. I am a decent person with a nice heart.

72. I commit to praising myself for who I am.

73. I am only critical of myself to the point where it is helpful.

74. Where ever I put focus and effort, I can see success.

75. I always hold on to my desires.

76. I consistently take action towards the realization of my dreams.

77. Everything that I try can work as long as I put work in.

78. My past does not hold any power over my present self-belief.

79. Everything that I need to accomplish my goals will come to me at the right moment.

80. Every opportunity can be an opportunity for advancement.

81. My high self-confidence will lead me down a very rewarding path of abundance.

82. I truly believe that all things will work themselves out for my benefit.

83. I am filled with courage and bravery.

84. My confidence results in an optimistic mindset in all situations.

85. I am at peace with my faith in myself and my abilities.

86. My confidence in myself strengthens and grows every single day.

87. I am an overcomer by nature.

88. I am a winner with a winner's mentality.

89. I possess infinite creative power and ability.

90. Right now, I am already a success.

91. I have no choice but to be successful.

92. Success is my only option.

93. My belief in myself inspires others to believe in themselves.

94. I inspire others around me to be the best version of who they are.

95. My potential is absolutely limitless.

96. I will never, ever quit.

97. I will never, ever give up.

98. I will never, ever stop short of my goals.

99. Persistence is an innate quality for me.

100. Perseverance is an innate quality for me.

101. Resilience is an innate quality for me.

102. I can adapt and overcome.

103. I am resourceful, and I always find the right tools, connections, and opportunities to better myself.

104. I have the intellect to come up with new strategies for solving any problem.

105. Every situation is an opportunity to bring forth my very best.

106. I easily let go of old thoughts patterns that are holding me back from being my absolute best.

107. I easily let go of unhealthy beliefs that are holding me back from being my absolute best.

108. Whatever it is, I can do it.

109. Whatever I do, I can do well.

110. I have the strength to make positive change.

111. I confidently make choices that will improve my life.

112. I have a positive mindset that benefits me in everything I do.

113. I am bold and confident.

114. I am optimistic and fearless.

115. I am in control of my life.

116. I am in control of myself.

117. I have the power to make things better.

118. I confidently embrace all of my imperfections.

119. I was born to be a success.

120. Everything that I do is aligned with my highest potential.

121. My confidence and belief in myself are always growing.

122. I am decisive and make good decisions with confidence.

123. My belief in who I am gives me motivation and energy.

124. I grow day by day through the fuel that is my self-confidence.

125. I move through my life with high self-confidence, and make and execute plans accordingly.

126. Doing my best comes easily to me.

127. I always act from an empowered place of confidence.

128. I always act from an empowered place of abundance.

129. I always act from an empowered place of strength.

130. Greatness is always my result.

131. I am willing and able to do whatever I need to do to see my dreams to fruition.

132. Feeling great about who I am is natural for me.

133. Doing my absolute best is all that I need to succeed.

134. I know that there are no limits on my success.

135. I know that there is no ceiling on my future.

136. I always act out of respect for myself no matter what.

137. I look forward to the amazing future that I have in store.

138. My best is yet to come.

139. I am loveable, and I am loved.

140. I will always make it to the other side.

141. I am a very self-disciplined person who knows how to accomplish what I want.

142. Making mistakes is normal, and I will not beat myself up over it.

143. I turn every mistake into a triumph.

144. I transform every negative into a positive.

145. I am a special being with talents that only I can express.

146. I believe in my ability to reach my desired outcome, no matter what things may look like.

147. My self-confidence is contagious and magnetic.

148. I will inevitably reach my highest potential.

149. I believe in the power of my dreams.

150. My confidence increases each and every single day.

151. I will always do what I set out to do, no excuses.

152. My confidence is unwavering.

153. I only seek to be my best self.

154. I have an immeasurable amount of potential for growth.

155. Today, I commit to building my self-confidence to even greater heights.

156. The more belief I have in who I am, the more other people believe in me.

157. I am entirely content with my skin and appearance.

158. I am totally at ease in my own skin.

159. Each day, I discover more about who I am and what is possible for me.

160. I take consistent productive action, and it is leading me to positive results.

161. Through my confidence, there is no limit on what I can accomplish.

162. Other people see my confidence as a part of who I am.

163. I can succeed in any environment.

164. I am very proud of my growth and excited about my prosperous future.

165. I am intelligent and skilled, but I know there is always more room for growth.

166. I am as confident in my personal morals and values and I am in my personal strengths and talents.

167. I always act in accordance with my ethics.

168. I am confident in my abilities, but I do not hold myself to impossible standards.

169. I love where I am and where I am going.

170. I am committed to moving ahead at my own unique pace.

171. I am unaffected by people who challenge my self-worth.

172. My self-discipline is an expression of my self-confidence in what I am striving to achieve.

173. All of my success flows from my confidence.

174. I have control over my life's outcomes and I take that control with confidence and boldness.

175. I possess the mental strength to get through anything.

176. I have the emotional resilience to come out the other side of any situation.

177. I am strong enough to turn any situation.

178. No matter what is happening, there is always something I can do to make it better.

179. I have the wisdom to choose what is best for me.

180. I have the mental clarity to make wise decisions in life and work.

181. Daily positive habits of thought continually lead me towards my best and most confident self.

182. I find confidence in my uniqueness.

183. Only I can express my gifts in my own special way.

184. My self-worth is determined by my identity inside, not my successes or failures.

185. I draw confidence from all the times that I persevered through hardships.

186. Momentary setbacks don't crush my self-esteem or confidence.

187. I will always remain committed to personal development.

188. I can achieve anything, even if it is beyond my grasp.

189. I have the persistence to overcome resistance.

190. Resistance in pursuit of my dreams is inevitable, and so is my ability to get past it.

191. Nobody can determine or limit who I am and what I am capable of accomplishing in this life.

192. I start each and every day by establishing my confidence and belief in myself.

193. When challenged, I stay committed to my values and my personal belief in myself.

194. My views and opinions matter and are held in high esteem by everyone around me.

195. I am confident enough to say no to situations or pressures that are not best for me.

196. I am not obligated to give in to other people's demands for my time and energy.

197. Though I am skilled and knowledgeable, I know when to seek help.

198. My confidence in myself makes it easy for me to share love with others.

199. I am a naturally positive person, fully aware of what I can accomplish.

200. I am always discovering new personal skills and talents.

201. All things are possible for me simply because I believe it to be so.

202. I have an ocean of creative ability within me.

203. I am confident enough to let go of anything or anyone that is not helpful for me.

204. Endless miracles are manifesting in my life.

205. I can express who I am easily and I have faith in my talent.

206. I always attract the very best of situations, people and opportunities.

207. I am brave, and my personal power is unlimited.

208. I am the creator of my own circumstances.

209. I have a steadfast faith in my innate abilities.

210. I will face and overcome all of my fears.

211. I handle pressure with focus, clarity, and calmness.

212. I always find the motivation needed to push through difficulties and pressure.

213. I am living out my highest calling for my life.

214. All of the prosperity and abundance that I crave is on the other side of my fears.

215. I have available to me limitless opportunities to advance my career.

216. My confidence in myself always shines through in an obvious way to others.

217. I am surrounded by new opportunities for advancement in my career.

218. My belief in myself makes me a great leader and motivator.

219. I am confident enough to accept what I cannot change.

220. I always feel a strong sense of calm and focus when taking on a new challenge.

221. I have no problem recognizing and working to improve my flaws.

222. Others are amazed by how easily I handle tough situations.

223. I immediately squash negative thoughts before they have the chance to grow bigger.

224. I will create a beautiful life for myself.

225. I can take on any leadership role with ease and comfort.

226. My self-confidence allows me to stand out from others.

227. My success and upward mobility are inevitable.

228. My mind is growing stronger each and every day.

229. I am a continual source of inspiration for others on how to believe strongly in who you are.

230. I always operate out of abundance, strength, security, and positivity.

231. I consciously let go of habits that are no longer serving me in my life.

232. I am ready for any challenge that comes my way.

233. I take consistent and deliberate actions that bring me closer to my goals.

234. Through my profound self-confidence, I continue to live my life with purpose and motivation.

235. My confidence always gives me a chance to make a comeback.

236. I understand that life is a journey, and I am always growing.

237. Every word I speak comes from a confident and capable version of myself.

238. My past failures are nothing but fuel for my future successes.

239. I can adapt to or change any circumstance.

240. As my beliefs about myself change, my world and experience also begin to change.

241. My potential has no limits.

242. I will accomplish whatever I desire.

243. Success is so easily drawn to me because I believe in myself.

244. I always bounce back from disappointments with even more confidence because it just makes me more determined.

245. I enjoy new challenges because it is an opportunity to sharpen my self-confidence.

246. I choose to live in confidence over fear.

247. Today, I am declaring victory over my circumstances and everything that I face.

248. I walk into each day with the expectation of success and high achievement.

249. Establishing good habits is easy for me.

250. Eradicating bad habits is easy for me.

251. My confidence is obvious to others in the way that I carry myself.

252. I always walk around with my head held high.

253. Every step I take gets me closer to my ultimate destiny.

254. Amazing things lie ahead for me.

255. I confidently take the reins in my life to take control of my future.

256. My self-esteem is a source of optimism in the face of setbacks.

257. I choose to see myself as the best version of myself and I know that in time I will get there.

258. I have strong and beneficial habits that steer me closer in the direction of my goals.

259. I never operate out of desperation because I know my value.

260. I have an inner compass that I trust to guide me to the right decisions.

261. I believe in myself and all that I am able to do.

262. I am prepared and destined to succeed.

263. I put forth excellence because I am worthy of excellence.

264. Extremely high levels of success await me.

265. I have an endless amount of positive qualities and talents.

266. I know I am a winner on the inside and the world can see it on the outside.

267. I ignore naysayers and simply continue moving along my own unique path.

268. My priorities are strongly in place, and I trust myself to follow through and commit to them.

269. I am solely responsible for the way I feel.

270. I have the self-assurance to give credit and praise to other people in my life where credit and praise are due.

271. The way that I talk to myself will always be positive and kind.

272. I remain confident in myself even when I see others succeed.

273. I have a "can do" and a "will do" attitude in pursuit of my dreams.

274. I have a champion's mindset and a winning belief system.

275. I perform well under pressure.

276. Everything I have to offer serves a unique and excellent purpose.

277. I move excitedly in the direction of nervousness because it means I am challenging myself to grow.

278. I have full confidence that everything difficult now will soon get easier in the future.

279. My lowest moments are not a reflection of who I truly am.

280. I am able to release my anxiety with confidence and focus on the moment.

281. I fully accept responsibility for all of my actions.

282. I have no problem apologizing for my mistakes and admitting my faults.

283. My confidence allows me to see the best in every single circumstance.

284. I am strong in the face of loss because I know ultimately things are working out for my benefit.

285. I am capable of leading myself and leading others to success.

286. The best things will come to me at the right time and at the right moment.

287. I have the skill to gracefully handle inner conflict.

288. I have the skill to gracefully handle external conflict.

289. What other people say about me does not shape who I am.

290. I am not the sum of other people's opinions.

291. Only I have the power to mold my self-image and self-worth.

292. I do what I say, and I say what I mean.

293. I am confident in what I bring to the table in all situations.

294. My self-assurance shows itself nonverbal and verbal ways.

295. There is a reason for everything and I know that there is a greater purpose for me.

296. I accept my circumstances as they are, as I work to change the parts I can control.

297. When people try to tear me down with their words, it only makes me better.

298. When people try to tear me down with their actions, it only makes me better.

299. I am able to consistently perform at my best regardless of how I fool.

300. I can change my thoughts and feelings at any time.

301. I can be confident in any and every situation I choose.

302. The confidence I have in myself makes other people confident in me.

303. My belief in myself is strong enough to withstand criticism from others.

304. I am in control of my thoughts, and, therefore, I am in control of my actions.

305. I am in control of my actions, and, therefore, I am in control of my outcomes.

306. I am in control of my outcomes, and, therefore, I am in control of my life.

307. I always make plans in expectation of a positive future.

308. I refuse to settle in any area of my life.

309. I visualize my future self as an unstoppable success.

310. The more confident I feel, the easier it is to be confident.

311. I have unstoppable momentum in the direction of my goals.

Chapter 21
Affirmations for Increasing Productivity and Improving Decision Making

Close your eyes. Imagine you're in a room where things are everywhere. It's supposed to be a bedroom, but with every single surface and furniture item covered, it's hard to tell. All around the room are heaps of filthy clothing in every corner, empty boxes on the floor, dirty dishes strewn about, a ball of wrinkled bedding on top of an unmade bed, unorganized paperwork covering the surface of what is intended to be a work desk, and everything is disorganized and out of control.

Everywhere you look, you see something that's supposed to be clean, folded, in a closet, or in a drawer. But it's not. And this is the room that you must sleep in and do work in. How does it make you feel? Stressed? Overwhelmed? Irritable? Confused? When our space is cluttered, it's hard to get things done and even harder to think straight. Our brains are no different.

Modern times have countless things constantly competing for our attention, demanding our focus, and ultimately taking up our mental space: calls, text messages, social media, phone notifications, pop-ups, media, news, and advertisements, just to name a few. And that's on top of the concerns and responsibilities that go along with everyday life. All of this together contributes to the cacophony of noise in our heads. With all these things constantly swirling through our brains, it's no wonder that focus and productivity are so difficult to achieve, and brain fog has seemingly become the norm.

Having a clear understanding of what to do but being unable to do it for whatever reason may be quite frustrating. You can't manage to keep your gaze fixed on the work at hand long enough to focus and accomplish it. You are unable to make choices since your mental clarity is insufficient. You are unable to be productive. Your low level of productivity has a negative impact on your self-esteem. You are unable to find mental tranquility. The next thing that's going to happen, not happen, or go wrong is clouding your ability to think clearly and rationally.

How can you mentally get back on track? By taking time away from all the noise and reprogramming your brain and resetting your mindset to make you feel calm, confident, optimistic, focused, and productive.

Your mindset makes all the difference. We often don't even realize the psychological and practical damage being done by disempowering negative thoughts rooted in our subconscious. In addition to causing feelings of helplessness and hopelessness that ding your self-confidence, negative thoughts also make you not want to take action towards your goals, a surefire way to eliminate all chance of success. That's why training your brain with intention can easily be the difference between attaining success and happiness, and not attaining success and happiness.

The use of affirmations is a highly efficient method of doing this. Affirmations can quite literally rewire your mind by physically affecting the neural pathways in your brain. Affirmations, when spoken coupled with the feeling one would feel if they honestly believed them to be true can be extremely powerful tools in improving and changing your life.

The Affirmations

1. Whatever I need to do, I do it now because the only time I have is the present moment.

2. My best future begins today with my current actions.

3. I am confident because I keep my promises to myself.

4. I like the satisfaction I get from accomplishing a job that I set out to achieve.

5. I do not give in to fear disguised as procrastination.

6. I am a well of wisdom, getting wiser every day.

7. I am clear on where I'm going, and clear on how to get there.

8. I make decisions based on my ultimate vision.

9. I prioritize what's necessary for the future over what's easy for right now.

10. I am okay feeling uncomfortable now so that I can feel comfortable later.

11. I unapologetically say no to things that are not in line with my goals and vision for myself.

12. I unapologetically say no to people that are not in line with my goals and vision for myself.

13. Although I am unstoppable, I take rest when needed.

14. I know the distinction between well-needed rest and laziness.

15. The sooner I complete a task, the sooner it is off my mind.

16. I am always learning from people about how to be more productive in my job.

17. I do what's best for me, without worrying about other people's opinions.

18. My environment is clean and organized, and supports my productivity.

19. I start today because some day never comes.

20. I focus on my personal priorities without guilt or shame.

21. I maintain simplicity in all areas of my life, which keeps my mind clear.

22. I am always growing and transforming for the better through the changes of life.

23. If I just start a project, the "how" always comes to me.

24. I do not need to know all the answers to get started.

25. My confidence, curiosity, and problem-solving skills show me that I have the ability to learn as I go along.

26. I work quickly and efficiently towards my goals.

27. I am able to stay focused on the task in front of me until it is complete.

28. I intuitively break down larger tasks into smaller, manageable pieces to avoid overwhelm.

29. I always have a clear list of things I need to get done.

30. I keep my mind clear by keeping my to do list on paper, not in my head.

31. I recruit the assistance of others to achieve my objectives.

32. I am a master delegator.

33. I'm proud of myself because I do what I say I'm going to do.

34. I can remain focused on the task at hand even in a room full of distractions.

35. My focus comes from within and I can tap into it where ever I go.

36. I maintain a distraction free work zone.

37. I know that when I really want to get something done, I can finish any task.

38. I'm not one to get mired down in the finer points.

39. I find it easy to zero in on something that needs doing.

40. I never spend too much time on a single task.

41. I know when it is time to move forward to the next step.

42. I know how to let good enough be good enough, and move on.

43. I pay attention to detail while maintaining my momentum.

44. I find it easy to focus on the target I have set for myself.

45. I can easily shift focus when necessary to accommodate changes while maintaining momentum.

46. My focus is unbreakable.

47. I put in the work now for the benefit of my future self.

48. I naturally know what to do to make my workflow more efficient.

49. Through the power of delegation, I am able to get many tasks completed at the same time.

50. I always maintain a high quality of work, no matter the caliber of task before me.

51. I can think my way out of any difficult problem.

52. I work with people who share my commitment to competence and excellence.

53. My work environment is full of great people who are dedicated to good work and success.

54. When I grow weary, I am grateful to have a team of people I can rely on.

55. I know there is more than one way to skin a cat so I do not get hung up on one particular strategy.

56. I quickly and seamlessly adapt to changes in strategy.

57. If something does not work, I quickly move on without missing a beat.

58. My diligence and focus serve as a great example to others.

59. I am productive, but I enjoy my work at the same time.

60. I do what's best for the long term, not just the short term.

61. Once I get the ball rolling, I become unstoppable.

62. My attention is only on what I am working on in this exact moment.

63. When a project gets started, it becomes easier for me to gain momentum in other projects.

64. My success in one area of my life helps me to have success in other areas of my life.

65. Getting items crossed off my to-do list is one of my favorite feelings.

66. I am a master of getting things done.

67. I feel calm when I am focused.

68. I pick and choose what projects and events are best for me to take on, rather than saying yes to everything.

69. When I set a goal, I move forward with confidence even though I may not know everything.

70. Perfectionism is just another form of procrastination.

71. I don't need all the answers to take the first step.

72. I know how and when to say no, which prevents me from spreading my time and energy too thin.

73. My body is my most important tool for a healthy, successful life so I take great care of it.

74. I think fast on my feet and solve unexpected problems quickly.

75. I am a quick critical thinker and can always find the right solution.

76. I am able to collaborate with different types of personalities to achieve the task at hand.

77. When I start something, I finish it.

78. The answers to my problems unfold as I take action.

79. I live a life driven by my commitments, not my emotions.

80. When it comes to time management, I am a dependable and prompt individual.

81. I make fast decisions, allowing me to work efficiently towards the goal at hand.

82. I finish what I start.

83. My future is decided by the work I put in now.

84. My future is decided by the decisions I make now.

85. I have the power to commit to a project and see it through until the very end.

86. I have my own system of organization that works wonders for me.

87. I prioritize proper sleep and healthy eating to give my mind and body sufficient fuel.

88. I always wake up with a plan for the day and execute accordingly.

89. I am known for my follow through.

90. I am known for my ceaseless dedication.

91. My excellent work ethic is well-known among my peers.

92. I cherish my time and make good use of it.

93. I value my energy and use it wisely.

94. I have a natural talent for managing my time wisely so that I complete everything I set out to do.

95. My time is valuable, and I spend it in a way that aligns with my life goals.

96. I know when it is time to start a project, when it is time to shift and when it is time to stop.

97. I am successful because I find it easy to balance my commitments.

98. I know how to make observations to see what is working, so I can do more of it.

99. I know how to make observations to see what is not working, so I can do less of it.

100. I always leave myself ample to time to complete the task at hand.

101. I eliminate unnecessary stress by starting projects early.

102. I am conscious of not taking on so much to where I compromise what is already on my plate.

103. I am aware of the areas I can improve on and do my best to get better.

104. When I feel like I hit a wall, I keep pushing until I get through it.

105. I am proactive about making changes in my schedule as needed to ensure both my productivity and my happiness.

106. I am aware enough to know when I need to do something and when someone else can be delegated to do something.

107. It feels good to sometimes trust others to make decisions.

108. My time is my most important commodity, and I do everything in my power to protect its value.

109. My discipline allows me to resist temptation when something important needs finishing.

110. As soon as I know all the information I need for the next step, I make a decision and act with haste.

111. I am 100% clear on what I want out of life.

112. I don't have to feel pressured to make every decision immediately.

113. If something comes up that I don't yet know how to approach, it is okay to take some time to find a solution.

114. I know how to be patient with myself when needed and act with urgency when needed.

115. Success may be achieved via a variety of means, and I want to discover my own without regard for the views of others.

116. Action and momentum will get me to my goal. Perfection and over-planning will not.

117. I deserve to rest without guilt after periods of productive work.

118. I put in the work to create the future I want and deserve.

119. What I put in, I will get out.

120. I know what I want and know how to achieve whatever I set my mind on.

121. I only focus on whichever task is in front of me at that moment.

122.   I speak up for myself when I want or need something.

123.   I listen to my intuition and trust it to guide me to the best decisions for me.

124.   I know when it is time to consult another person in order to work through an obstacle quickly, efficiently, and confidently.

125.   Though I sometimes seek the counsel of others, ultimately the final say is mine.

126.   Just because other people don't agree with my decision, it doesn't make it wrong.

127.   There is profound wisdom in me and all around me that helps me make solid decisions.

128.   I am confident that I will make the right choice.

129.   I am capable of making difficult decisions within a reasonable amount of time.

130.   I know how long is too long to deliberate on a decision.

131.   I approach new choices with confidence.

132.   I know how to make decisions that are mutually beneficial to everyone involved.

133.   I make decisions with logic and empathy.

134.   I am capable of finding a good balance between rational thinking and creative thinking.

135.   I am determined to complete what I have started.

136.   I take my commitments seriously.

137. I am capable of finding my way through difficult tasks.

138. When I do my best, I can let go, knowing I did all I could do.

139. I am a leader and can guide myself and others toward success.

140. I revel in the sense of accomplishment I feel when I finish a project.

141. My self-confidence and self-esteem increase with each project I finish.

142. I believe in my choices and stand by my decisions.

143. I am comfortable with making important decisions.

144. I welcome criticism with grace and take action on the feedback I receive.

145. I am self-aware and conscious enough to know what I need to do next.

146. I am intentional about my actions and make each move with progress in mind.

147. I will pass through this day with intent.

148. I know what I want out of my life and know what it takes to get there.

149. I have reasonable expectations of myself and others.

150. I know what matters most to me, and choose to focus my time and energy on that alone.

151. I don't have to do everything, I only do what matters.

152. I work more efficiently when I am well-rested, so I make good sleep a priority.

153. My healthy routines are essential to my ability to focus.

154. If I have an "off day," I know I can get back on track tomorrow.

155. I place boundaries around my work time so I can get things done.

156. I place boundaries around my work space so I can get things done.

157. It's more important for me to keep moving forward than to be perfect.

158. There is a time to think, and there is a time to act.

159. There is no such thing as perfect.

160. I am greatly rewarded for my discipline.

161. I am capable of creating excellent projects and products in my work and business.

162. I have a habit of excellence.

163. I succeed in everything I do.

164. I reap the benefits from my dedication to my commitments.

165. I do what it takes to see things through to the end so I can get the results I desire.

166. It's better to be imperfect in motion than to be perfect and still.

167. I am respected, revered, and sought after by my professional peers.

168. I am known for delivering consistently great results in my work.

169. I work smart, not just hard.

170. I do not have to do everything; I get help when I need it.

171. There are people who are ready and willing to help me with my problems, and I attract them easily.

172. I have great intuition for knowing what step to do next.

173. I trust my instincts and believe they will guide me to success.

174. Everything is solvable.

175. I make changes in my life for the better every day.

176. I get closer and closer to greatness with every step I take.

177. My organizational skills help me maintain control over my life.

178. I feel strong because I do what I set out to do.

179. I only focus on today's work, today.

180. I leave tomorrow's work for tomorrow.

181. I become more and more clear on my direction as I grow and learn from my mistakes as well as my successes.

182. I achieve more when I move forward with an imperfect plan, than when I don't move with a perfect plan.

183. I appreciate my work ethic and my ability to problem solve.

184. I can solve problems quickly, efficiently, and effortlessly.

185. I can quickly troubleshoot my way around any obstacle that comes up.

186. I become more and more clear on what I want as each day passes.

187. I can and will do whatever it takes to fulfill my destiny.

188. I will get out what I put in.

189. When something comes up that I haven't experienced before, I am patient with myself as I come up with a solution.

190. When I am stuck, I enlist the help of others more skilled than me.

191. I am skilled at finding people whose strengths supplement my weaknesses.

192. I know what I need and I trust what I know.

193. I am great at coming up with strategy and deciding the best next step forward.

194. I have the power to create new and innovative things.

195. I trust in my ability to make decisions that lead to productivity and prosperity.

196. I work actively on what I can control and release all cares about what I cannot.

197. I wake up every day, renewing and honoring my commitments to myself.

198. Action is the best source of motivation, so now I am an action taker.

199. I always move forward confidently on my projects and goals.

200. Ideas show up when I do, so I show up to put my work in towards my goals.

201. I am an endless well of creative ideas.

202. I have a calm mind, so solutions easily come to me.

203. I trust my plan of action, and move forward with confidence.

Chapter 22
Affirmations for Success

Having objectives is one thing, but achieving goals is quite another thing entirely. You may have the strong desire to quit abusing drugs for instance, learn a new skill, or become compassionate, but you may discover that those desires never become a reality. You will feel dissatisfied, helpless and unhappy because it is our natural inclination to grow. Creating the kind of life you want based on your core values strengthens your self-esteem.

Accepting yourself becomes easier when you are able to create changes and achieve your goals. As someone who is still struggling with poor self-esteem, you may keep finding reasons not to put in the amount of effort required like a lack of time, adequate information, or believing that success is out of reach. You can overcome these stumbling blocks by doing the following:

1. Make adequate plan

You will get confused or overwhelmed by the steps you have to take to reach your goals if you dive straight into them without a sufficient plan. Achieving your goal become easier when you take time to analyze and break it down into bits - the steps that will help you arrive. What are the skills, experience, resources or equipment you will need and how can you get them? Answering questions like these will make for a better plan and prevent you from getting stuck, frustrated, or confused halfway through achieving your goal.

2. Gather essential information

Of course, there is no way you can successfully achieve a goal if you lack the basic knowledge needed. However, stop using this as an excuse when you can find the necessary information by simply searching for it.

Sign up for training, find a mentor, read books, or carry out research on the internet.

3. Manage your time properly

Even if you gather essential information and make adequate plans, you will still be unable to achieve your goals if you never have extra time on your hands. What activities do you engage in every day? Take stock of your daily activities; you may find yourself guilty of allowing tasks that are less important overshadow the important ones.

Learn to prioritize: take care of the most important tasks first and leave the least important ones for later. For instance, you could move painting the house to the bottom of your to-do list and ascribe number one position to helping your kids with their homework. Creating a list of your daily tasks will help you know which ones to do away with to make space for better goals.

Another important (really) skill to develop is the ability to say no. Sort the requests into categories depending upon their urgency or reasonableness.

4. Imagine the worst

When you find yourself giving in to the fear of failure by not making any substantial effort to achieve your goal, ask yourself: "what's the worst that could happen?" So, you acquire the job and get fired in a matter of weeks because they discover that you are a flop, or you summon the courage to go on stage and give a presentation but end up not making any sense. Okay, that's the worst that could happen! You don't know for sure how it will turn out until you try. Besides, what if you lose the job? You get another job.

5. Stop trying to be perfect

You really should stop trying to be perfect. Remember that mistakes are inevitable and do not add to or take away your self-worth unless you let them. Do what you can at the moment, one step at a time. Hold on to your core values and don't give in to the pressure of living by other people's standards.

You can also apply the following techniques in addition to the above tips:

- **Visualize that you've already achieved your goals:** Practice visualizing the way you will look and act when you've achieved your goals. Create scenes in your mind in which you are in a satisfying relationship, no longer an alcoholic, learning how to code, have lost 50 pounds, more confident and doing whatever it is you want to. The act of visualization reprograms the negative way you see yourself in your mind and causes you to act out what you already have in your subconscious. Believe it or not, visualization is a very effective tool you can use to bring yourself closer to achieving your dreams. Remember poor self-esteem stems from seeing yourself as lesser than other human beings. It never crosses your mind for once that you are equal, so you keep choosing negative routes and negative people. Visualizing yourself differently can change it all.

    How do you practice visualization? By simply finding a quiet spot that you can let yourself relax and simply breathe. Focus on breathing and playing the scenes you planned to visualize. Imagine yourself doing whatever you usually do every day—waking up, brushing your teeth and so on and then see yourself taking small, positive steps to achieve your goals. Definitely, distracting thoughts will come. The trick is to observe those thoughts without pursuing them and refocusing on the positive picture.

    Practice visualization at least twice a day, once in the morning and at night before you sleep.

- **Have someone who will be checking up on you**: Another helpful technique is to share your short or long-term goals with a friend or family member and ask them to check up on you every week or so. Let the person know the steps you have to take to reach your goals as well as the timeframe that each step will demand. You will be driven to stay committed to your goals as you will want to have a progressive report to give that friend or family member every week.

The Affirmations

1. I am constantly working hard and building my skill set to advance my professional success.

2. I do not judge my level of success by the amount of money I make, but rather by the level of satisfaction I have with my life.

3. I do not measure my success by the amount of money I earn, but the quality of people with which I surround myself.

4. I have a healthy work-life balance that promotes my mental and emotional health.

5. I show initiative and dedication by arriving to work early every day.

6. I possess the resiliency and fortitude to recover from my mistakes and move forward.

7. I enhance my life with hobbies and leisure activities outside of work that make me happy.

8. I have the courage and capability to conquer all the challenges that come my way.

9. I easily remain focused on completing my daily tasks.

10. I always have opportunities to be successful because I do my best.

11. I challenge myself to improve a little each day, which increases my chances of success.

12. I do not allow the fear of failure to stop me from chasing my dreams.

13. I overcome excuses and do whatever it takes to achieve my goals.

14. All of my perceived handicaps are actually gifts that make me and my story unique.

15. I am not happy because I am successful, I am successful because I am happy.

16. I banish doubt and hesitation in favor of confidence and action.

17. I'm on a mission to become the greatest version of myself possible.

18. I know that things don't have to be perfect in order for me to be successful.

19. I keep my eyes on my prize no matter what is going on around me.

20. I dress for success because presenting a good appearance makes me feel good.

21. I make an effort to maintain a professional look so that I can always make a good first impression.

22. I practice the skills I want to hone a little each day, so I become more proficient.

23. I cast a wide net and broaden my horizons to explore the various available opportunities.

24. I set realistic and achievable goals for myself that I am accomplishing with ease and happiness.

25. I constantly expand my knowledge by learning more every day through reading and research.

26. I have the willpower and self-control to finish tasks even when they present challenges or stress.

27. I possess the wisdom and courage to make decisions that will improve my life.

28. I experience more success in my career when I possess a positive attitude.

29. I am consciously creating a happy, well-rounded, and productive life for myself.

30. My physical performance is at a peak when my mental performance is also.

31. I focus on being happy, which is a key factor in achieving success.

32. I do not quantify my success by the material possessions I own, but by the happiness that I feel.

33. I seek out interesting side projects that help keep my mind happy and productive outside of work.

34. I ensure my personal happiness first and foremost, and as a result, personal success easily follows.

35. I possess strong leadership qualities.

36. I have the capacity to make a positive impact in this world.

37. I am always learning, always growing, and always improving in every area of my life.

38. I have the drive to follow through on my ideas and finish what I start.

39. I devote my time and attention to concentrating on the measures that will enable me to reach my objectives.

40. I am an achiever in every area of life.

41. The more I have, the easier it is for me to get even more.

42. I trust, know, and believe that my hard work always pays off.

43. I know that if I work hard, wealth, prosperity, and abundance will be the result.

44. Each day, I discover new ways I can become more successful.

45. I can gain power and use it wisely to help others.

46. Regardless of the situation, I will always keep the door open for new chances.

47. I will never stop growing my wealth and prosperity.

48. It is important to me that I perceive the world through the eyes of an entrepreneur to guarantee that I never miss an opportunity to generate money.

49. My growing prosperity opens new doors to greater opportunity.

50. I work hard now knowing that there is unlimited success for me ahead.

51. I deserve wealth and abundance for the hard work I put in.

52. Everything that I try to do, I am able to excel in.

53. My relationships are just as full as my bank account.

54. I am in love with the life that I am leading.

55. I am blessed and successful beyond measure.

56. Seeing new opportunities is easy for me.

57. I generate what I want, when I want it, and in the manner that I want.

58. I have a life that is balanced, whole, and amazing.

59. I am currently living my own personal definition of success.

60. I place no limits on what I can achieve and am willing to pay the price to get there.

61. I recognize that growth has a price and I am willing to pay it.

62. Abundance flows to me in unlimited amounts when I work hard to achieve it.

63. I can earn any amount of money I want by putting in the work.

64. I recognize opportunities and convert them into money and riches.

65. I am always on a quest for personal growth, which serves me in all areas of my life.

66. I move forward towards wealth without overthinking things.

67. I have a mind that is clear, alert, and focused, which helps me achieve success.

68. I have a well-rounded, successful life.

69. My mental peace is just as much an indicator of my success as my bank account.

70. Everything I do leads to more success for me.

71. I am proud of what I have achieved.

72. I can increase my streams of income whenever I so decide.

73. I multiply my success by working smarter, not harder.

74. We can all be wealthy if we work smart.

75. I always find a way to be successful no matter what.

76. My lifestyle is a reflection of the success I have attained.

77. Success is better when shared and I always find ways to share it.

78. I rejoice in the things I enjoy as a result of my work.

79. I spread happiness, joy, and abundance.

80. Helping others is always an opportunity for success and creating a better life.

81. I have everything it takes to seize every opportunity.

82. Every business I create will flourish because I will do what it takes to ensure that.

83. I am swift to action, and my bank account reflects that.

84. I'm living the life of my dreams thanks to the help of others.

85. I can afford anything I want because I have put in the work to build wealth.

86. I feel satisfied each day knowing I am working to secure my future.

87. Wealth and abundance are available in unlimited amounts for people like me who are willing to work for it.

88. I can build and create my dream home.

89. I can build and create my dream lifestyle.

90. I can build and create my dream life.

91. I am proud of the life that I have created for myself.

92. When I put in work, there is no limit to what I can achieve.

93. I grab opportunities and turn them into wealth magnets.

94. I am the kind of person who succeeds in everything I do.

95. I am comfortable with money and wealth because I've earned it.

96. At the end of the day, hard effort is always rewarded.

97. I can't lose because I do what it takes to win.

98. I am successful, resourceful, and efficient because I focus on solutions instead of dwelling on problems.

99. I constantly expose myself to new ideas, unique viewpoints, and different ways of approaching situations.

100. I am complementary and supportive of those who I work with.

101. I choose to focus on solving problems and finding solutions.

102. I effortlessly feed my body only with things that make me feel good, productive, and mentally alert.

103. Everything I put in my body makes me feel healthier and happier in life and work.

104. I have a clear vision and always maintain sight of my goals.

105. I easily come up with action plans to accomplish my goals successfully and effortlessly.

106. Whenever I'm faced with a problem I cannot yet solve, a mentor appears to help me through.

107. I solicit the counsel of experienced people who can help guide me on the right path.

108. I take pride in maintaining a professional, put together appearance.

109. I have control over the urge to procrastinate.

110. I effortlessly meet deadlines in a timely manner without stress or anxiety.

111. A significant part of my personal success is giving back to others in a positive, impactful way.

112. I communicate well with the people I work with.

113. All my goals are within reach.

114. I always seek the opportunity to learn and grow more within my field.

115. I am grateful to work with people I respect for their integrity.

116. I am grateful to work with people I admire for their achievements.

117. I use my talents to teach and help others to find success.

118. I follow bliss, not money.

119. I take pride in preparing and educating myself thoroughly so I can do my best.

120. I take advantage of opportunities for professional development without hesitation as they arise.

121. I constantly seek opportunities to further my education and knowledge in my career.

122. I love to get out of my own comfort zone because I know that is where growth happens.

123. I dream big and act fast.

124. My positive habit of regular physical activity has a positive impact on my work.

125. I have the ability to become the top, most successful person in my field.

126. My positive attitude allows me to get more work done—faster, better, and more efficiently.

127. My enthusiastic attitude drives my success in work and boosts my motivation.

128. I effortlessly remain focused and stay on task in my work.

129. I am proud of how far I have come on my professional journey, and I look forward to going even further.

130. I approach each day with purpose and passion.

131. I take charge of my life, and I take responsibility for its outcome.

132. I have the energy to work tirelessly to accomplish the goals that I set for myself.

133. I set a positive example for others through my strong work ethic.

134. I have a clear vision of my own personal version of success.

135. I consistently take the necessary steps for me to reach my goals.

136. My strong and effective communication skills contribute to my career success.

137. I embrace challenges fearlessly and never back down from them.

138. I am constantly checking off goals that I've achieved.

139. My consistent accomplishments make me feel happy, proud, and fulfilled.

140. I think ahead and plan wisely for long-term success in addition to short-term.

141. I put my full effort and energy into everything I do.

142. I keep up with innovation in my field so I can remain ahead of the curve.

143. I always master new technologies in my field so I can remain competitive.

144. I create a positive environment for those I work with.

145. My energy motivates people to work harder, which contributes to our collective success.

146. I usually surround myself with things that excite and inspire me to continue my journey.

147. My positivity boosts my energy levels and aids me in being more productive.

148. I am proud to have built a meaningful career that helps contribute to the happiness of others.

149. The advantages of having a happy view on life are continually being reaped in unexpected ways.

150. I devote my time to complete projects that I start, and my efforts are paying off.

151. I look forward to working and enjoy what I do.

152. I take advantage of my personal strengths to help me make progress every day.

153. I am unafraid to push myself and I respond well to professional challenges.

154. No matter what, I remain disciplined and keep my eyes on the prize.

155. I am capable of succeeding beyond my wildest imagination in any career path.

156. My hopeful and optimistic outlook makes it easy for opportunities to find me.

157. I am fueled by a sense of purpose, which ensures my success in my endeavors.

158. I feel like a success because I love every part of my life.

159. I commit myself fully to my projects until they are completed with excellence.

160. I am a go-getter, and I take action and go after the things I want in my life.

161. Whatever I see in my mind or visualize in my life, I can attract and attain.

162. I am constantly getting better every day because of my commitment to constant improvement.

163. I go for what I want and expect the best, regardless of the potential outcomes.

164. The success of others inspires and motivates me.

165. I have incredible self-discipline that causes success in every area of my life.

166. My good attitude and ambition move me closer to prosperity every day.

167. I happily put in time on a consistent basis to realize my goals.

168. My efforts are worth it, and I am constantly rewarded for my persistence.

169. I attain better results in my work by staying motivated.

170. I am surrounded by positive, encouraging people who want success as much as I do.

171. I have the ability to make wise decisions quickly and follow through with them quickly.

172. I stay on top of my work and start and finish things earlier than planned.

173. I have full faith and unshakeable confidence that I am able to achieve my goals.

174. I have wonderful friends, family, and relationships, which is its own success.

175. I trust my intuition and follow my gut instincts because they are always right.

176. I only see success in my future, and success is my only option.

177. My past achievements motivate me to keep pushing forward to achieve even greater things.

178. I keep my work space clear, which keeps my mental space clear for maximum productivity.

179. I make terrific first impressions on everyone I encounter because of my positive attitude.

180. I possess the necessary traits needed for upward mobility in society and life.

181. I am conscious of the way I mentally and emotionally approach every goal.

182. I know that my attitude has a direct correlation to my performance and outcome.

183. My positive attitude allows me to excel in endeavors both inside and outside of work.

184. I concentrate on big picture thinking and don't get held down by small details.

185. I always go above and beyond the call of duty, for which my efforts are always rewarded.

186. I lead by example and cultivate a positive culture in my workplace.

Chapter 23
Affirmations for Building, Keeping, and Growing Wealth

What makes the wealthy, wealthy? What makes the successful, successful? And why is it that the rich seem to get richer and the more successful people become even more successful? It all stems from the mind. Your actions will never go where your thoughts have not already been, and the fact is that wealthy people think differently. The millionaire mindset begins with a positive relationship with money and a positive view of money. It often requires eliminating the negative programming around money that has been put into our heads by our parents, friends, society, and the media....

"Money is the root of all evil."

"Rich people are dishonest and selfish."

"It's bad to want to be rich."

"There's not enough for everyone to be rich."

"Everyone who's rich either got lucky, cheated their way there, or was born that way."

"It's not possible for people like me to be rich."

Thoughts and embedded beliefs like these repel wealth and make it impossible to reach greater financial heights. Wealthy people know that the desire to be rich is simply the desire to maximize their potential, gain the resources to allow them and their loved ones to live their best lives. It can help those in need on a large scale in a way only money can do and provide products and services that are so valuable and helpful that consumers are happy to exchange money for them. The wealthy know that a healthy desire for money, a positive relationship with money, honest work, and proper stewardship over your finances is the best way to get there.

The road to wealth and success for most is often impeded by a poverty mentality shaped by unconscious programs in our minds. We are wired to carry out the ideas put in our heads a long time ago by outside influences. But a poverty mentality is not just about negative thoughts and beliefs about money. It is about being trapped with an "I can't" attitude. It's a thought process that often blames others for the present circumstances, whether your spouse, your boss, the president, or the economy.

Poverty is a state of mind, and people who remain in financial poverty are the type who always find reasons why they can't. They have an endless supply of excuses, stories about what they should have done, and rants about what they could have done if it weren't for some external force outside of themselves they blame for their shortcomings and unrealized dreams.

Successful people with the millionaire mindset take responsibility and control over themselves, their actions, and their outcomes, which in turn gives them control over their lives. While others talk about doing things, they take action and never blame others or external forces for their circumstances. They don't wait around for luck, the economy to turn around, that perfect business partner to walk into their lives, their bank account to magically double, etc. They change what they don't like and believe they can do so.

They are leaders, who take control and lead themselves, businesses, projects, and other people on the path towards success. They are decisive and like to be in control rather than sitting on the sidelines because they are actually very confident in their ability to make good decisions with positive outcomes.

Whether we like it or not, we are all leaders: it's just a matter of whether we are good or bad leaders. Leadership begins at home, so to be a leader, you need to be a leader of yourself first and foremost. This begins by becoming a master at your time management and owning your productivity. It also means taking pride in your work and bringing excellence to everything you do on every level, as you make your climb to the top, no matter who is looking.

People destined for success have good, foundational habits that they apply in their daily lives, whether that means showing up early to a meeting, being the first to volunteer for a task at work, or taking small daily action steps toward their entrepreneurial dreams. It is from these basic habitual actions and a foundational attitude that everything flows.

And while successful people make a lot of money, they know that material riches are not the only important type to have. They know that wealth reaches far beyond money alone. Success is about more than financial success. So they prioritize the people in their lives by balancing work with family, relationships, recreation, and their personal lives. They are cheerful givers with an attitude of service within their work, and an attitude of charity outside it.

Sometimes, it seems that we're doing all the right things and taking all the right actions to move toward our goals, but we still can't see progress. It is your frame of mind that makes all the difference. Disempowering ideas will make you feel powerless and hopeless, and they can be difficult to overcome. And since these negative beliefs are often anchored in our subconscious, we are often unaware of the psychological harm we are causing ourselves. But training your brain to be positive, optimistic, and expect good things to happen can be the difference between seeing success and not seeing it.

It's time to think big and stop being plagued and crippled by limiting beliefs. There is limitless potential and unlimited abundance for everyone who desires success and wealth. It is time to join those with the millionaire mindset. Hard work always pays off, and there are unlimited opportunities to create wealth. Anyone and everyone can become successful, including you.

It's time to adopt the thought processes of the rich and use affirmations to drive these thoughts into your subconscious. Affirmations will help you develop the right attitudes and habits for success. Because from new thoughts will spring new actions that will lead you on the right path to wealth in every area of your life.

The Affirmations

1. I have unlimited income potential.
2. I have multiple streams of income.
3. I make passive income as a result of the wise investment decisions I make.
4. I am creative and use my creativity to solve people's problems, generating wealth.
5. I act on my creative ideas and turn them into wealth.
6. I know that the only way to true wealth is not to trade my time for money.
7. I know that the only way to true wealth is providing value to the marketplace.
8. I know that the only way to true wealth is to sell valuable products and services.
9. I know that the only way to true wealth is to have my own business.
10. I love my business because it puts me in total control of my income.

11. I sell valuable products and services that improve people's lives.

12. Selling is good because it helps people to solve their problems.

13. Selling is good because it provides unlimited income potential for me.

14. My business allows me to choose what I do with my time.

15. I have financial security because I constantly have money coming in from multiple sources.

16. I leverage my time and the time of others to multiply my productivity.

17. I know there is only so much time in the day, so I have a team of people working towards my goals.

18. Wealth comes to me daily through various sources.

19. I can create wealth whenever I want or need to.

20. I have wealth that will take care of my family for generations.

21. I am a magnet for prosperity.

22. All of my efforts result in income.

23. I am completely deserving of all of the money I make.

24. My goals are in alignment with the creation of wealth and prosperity.

25. My mind is in alignment with the creation of wealth and prosperity.

26. My spirit is in alignment with the creation of wealth and prosperity.

27. My actions are in alignment with the creation of wealth and prosperity.

28. The more I get, the more I give.

29. The richer I get, the richer I make others.

30. I will improve the service I provide to humankind every single day.

31. I am determined to provide the best product or service that I possibly can.

32. I invest money back into my business to constantly grow it.

33. I invest money back into my business to constantly improve it.

34. My bank account is filled with money and always growing.

35. I can create wealth and money on command, by providing or improving the service I provide to others.

36. I fulfill the needs of others and generate wealth in the process.

37. I allow myself to receive as much wealth as I deserve, which is unlimited.

38. I create prosperity and share it with others.

39. Nothing will stop me from creating as much wealth as possible.

40. The more I give, the more I seem to get.

41. It is my joy to share my wealth.

42. Sharing my money makes it multiply.

43. I am grateful for the freedom that my business affords me.

44. Wealth is a state of mind, so even if restarting from nothing, I can always rebuild it.

45. I do not hoard money because through its use, I achieve prosperity and liberty.

46. I satisfy greater needs of the people and bring greater wealth into my life in return.

47. I generate wealth by helping people get what they want.

48. I expect to be paid in proportion to the service I provide others, and I will gladly provide that service.

49. My business allows me to live my ultimate lifestyle.

50. I live my life with a win-win philosophy and generate wealth in a way both my customers and I will benefit.

51. I only increase my prices when I increase the quality or value of the product or service I provide.

52. I always bring my absolute best to whatever I do.

53. Every single task or position deserves my best and that is what I bring.

54. I am open to receiving as much wealth as I am blessed with.

55. There is an infinite amount of wealth to go around.

56. I trust that my hard work will always pay off some way, some day.

57. I am grateful for every person who plays a role in making my dreams a reality.

58. I treat everyone with respect who helps contribute to the realization of my vision.

59. I am diligent and responsible with my income no matter what level it is right now.

60. I save and invest my money at all times, at all income levels.

61. I have no limits for my life and wealth.

62. I know that real wealth exists in the mind and those who have it can create it with ease even if all their money is taken from them.

63. I can create material wealth without limit.

64. Despite my financial success, I always have time and energy for my most cherished relationships and hobbies.

65. I have the knowledge to create real wealth at any time that I want.

66. I give back with abundance in amazing ways, and it returns to me ten-fold.

67. I have an entrepreneurial mindset and live independently on my own terms.

68. I am creative and create wealth and prosperity through the creative process.

69. I have the ability to profitably monetize all of my ideas.

70. I am wealthy because I turn the ideas in my head into action.

71. I am always wealthy because wealth is a state of mind.

72. I can create money at will because my abundance lies in my creativity.

73. My business allows me to live a life of my choosing.

74. I only compete with myself in improving my own products and services.

75. Every single day is an opportunity to serve others and create wealth in the process.

76. Wealth flows into my life continuously and effortlessly.

77. I have the wisdom to make profitable investments with my money.

78. Serving others through charity requires wealth, and I generate wealth to help the unfortunate.

79. We all have the right and ability to be wealthy; we just have to ask for it.

80. I speak up and make my needs and desires known, so I get them.

81. No matter the career, profession, or business I choose, I will rise to the top and be prosperous.

82. There are no limits to abundance, and everyone can be wealthy if they choose.

83. I choose to be wealthy and will provide service to others in return.

84. More money just makes you more of what you already are, and I am already kind and generous.

85. I deserve the money I receive because I serve others with love and without hesitation.

86. I deserve whatever I put in the work to earn.

87. The more money I make, the better because the more I can help myself and others.

88. As I grow myself on my personal development journey, my bank account grows.

89. Wealth is not a thing. It's a mindset, and I have the mindset of wealth, which can never be taken away from me.

90. I can grow wealth at any time and place, and the amount of my choosing.

91. I am proud of being rich.

92. I love being rich, and I use my riches to help others.

93. I am always attracting huge amounts of money into my life.

94. I always have an abundance of money because I have an abundance mindset.

95. I always have enough money to meet and exceed my personal financial obligations.

96. I will not be stopped in my quest to shamelessly create as much money as I want.

97. Gaining wealth is a good thing that benefits me and others.

98. Being wealthy allows me to help those in need on a massive scale.

99. I will move past any obstacle that prevents me from earning as much wealth as possible.

100. It's okay to value money and want more of it.

101. I expect to grow with each new project I embark upon.

102. I constantly expect bigger and better things in my life.

103. The system is rigged in my favor and the world wants me to be rich.

104. I seize opportunities that come my way with both hands.

105. I use the wealth I generate to generate even more wealth for me.

106. I give myself permission to become rich and successful in every area of life.

107. Constant growth requires constant change, and I am willing to pay that price.

108. How rich I am inside directly correlates to how rich I am outside.

109. My capacity to grow and expand in every way is unlimited.

110. Through wealth, I create abundance, and through abundance, I create freedom.

111. I freely share the knowledge of how to become wealthy with others.

112. I accept money into my life because I deserve it.

113. I already own all of the resources necessary to generate money in abundance.

114. I can create unlimited prosperity and the choice to do so is mine.

115. I am grateful for the talents and traits I have that allow me to build unlimited amounts of wealth.

116. No person, thing, circumstance, or obstacle will ever stop me from achieving my goal of wealth.

117. Money is available to anyone who seeks it.

118. I attract others who share my wealth mindset and we support each other in creating unlimited abundance.

119. I have the ability to recognize opportunities where others perceive challenges, which enables me to earn money when others are unable to do so.

120. I consciously remove any obstacles, physical or mental, to wealth and prosperity.

121. I consciously remove any obstacles, real or imagined, to wealth and prosperity.

122. I applaud the success of others and use it as inspiration for what is possible for me.

123. I think big and believe I can do anything I put my mind to.

124. I admire the successful and seek to emulate what they do to create my own success.

125. I respect those who are able to earn their own wealth and become rich.

126. I seek to be like those who are self-sufficient and create wealth on command.

127. Making money can be easy and doesn't have to be hard.

128. I am willing to put in the work to become rich, no matter how easy or hard it turns out to be.

129. I have a positive attitude about money and love it without shame.

130. Big life changes are opportunities to make big life changes.

131. When life brings change, it brings with it an opportunity for me to grow in every way.

132. I love unexpected change because it forces me to increase in every area of my life.

133. Money is an amplifier—if I am sincere and good, I will only become more so.

134. Everyone has the right to become wealthy, myself included.

135. Money is not the root of all evil, it is the generator of all wealth.

136. My ability to generate wealth is without limit.

137. No matter how much wealth I generate, I always help others to become rich with me.

138. It is a human right to become wealthy, but only I can exercise that right.

139. Being rich, wealthy, and abundant is in alignment with my spiritual beliefs.

140. I owe it to my creator to become and achieve all that I can, making use of the gifts I have been given.

141. They are unlimited resources out there to help me become wealthy.

142. I will never stop my service to mankind and therefore will always receive wealth in return.

143. I will never stop loving humankind, and being generous with my wealth.

144. I am not ashamed of making money.

145. I do not need to shamefully hide my success, because it can serve as a motivator to others.

146. When people see my success, it opens their eyes to what is possible for them.

147. My mind is always focused on the positive things money can bring.

148. I do not love money for its own sake, but for the positive things it can do for myself and others.

149. I am persistent and will overcome any obstacle that stands in the way of my financial future.

150. I am creative enough to always find quick, creative solutions to apparent problems in my business.

151. All of my actions are in congruence with my financial goal of attaining wealth.

152. I believe in myself and in my own capacity to generate wealth and prosperity.

153. Those who envy me only fuel me even more toward my goals of success.

154. Those who doubt me only fuel me even more toward my goals of success.

155. I follow the examples of others who are already living the life I want to live.

156. I accept the fact that those who are wealthier must be providing more value.

157. The confidence I need to create wealth is already within me.

158. I am proud of the product or service I provide to others in exchange for money.

159. I don't make excuses when obstacles show up in my path towards my goals.

160. Other people's negativity does not deter me from reaching my goals.

161. What others perceive as limits on them has nothing to do with me.

162. I set my own personal possibilities, not the opinions of others.

163. As I master my ability to generate wealth on command, I give back by teaching others what I know.

164. I love sharing knowledge and I love sharing wealth.

165. Money is the root of all prosperity.

166. I have a burning passion for growing my business.

167. The money I earn allows me to enjoy all the amazing things life has to offer.

168. Liberty is my most prized possession, and money is the most powerful way to preserve it.

169. I am dedicated to becoming all I can in life and in business.

170. I grow my money through wise investment decisions.

171. I gravitate towards those who are successful and admire the wealth and abundance they create.

172. Those who provide value to others deserve the money and success they receive in return.

173. Persistence pays off and I am a persistent person in pursuit of my goals.

174. I never give up when I am pursuing what is good and just.

175. Money obtained in the service of others is good and well-deserved.

176. I am willing to do the work required to change my family's financial future for the better.

177. Every day, I do something that gets me closer to achieving the success and abundance I desire.

178. I enjoy working when work it is in the service of others.

179. I enjoy earning money when I know it is in response to my service of others.

180. I deserve the rewards that come in return of giving service and value to others.

181. I have definite clear plans that will lead to my goal of generating wealth and abundance.

182. I fully commit to my plan to generate wealth and abundance.

183. I pursue my good ideas so they turn into money for me and value for others.

184. I am resourceful and always find answers to any questions I have.

185. I am resourceful enough to always be able to find a solution to any problem.

186. I am always able to seek and find the help I need when obstacles arise.

187. The attainment of wealth is possible at any age, no matter how young or old.

188. Everywhere I look, I see opportunities conspiring to help me achieve my goals of success.

189. I see ways of making money all around me, all the time.

190. I am building an empire of wealth that will give me all the money I need and help me enrich the lives of others.

191. I am capable of generating all the money I will ever need.

192. I am creative, happy, and living in a world of unlimited abundance.

193. I effortlessly find money-making opportunities.

194. I am limitless and unstoppable when it comes to getting rich.

195. I am rich not just in finances, but also in my relationships.

196. When I perceive an opportunity to earn money, I jump at the chance to seize it.

197. I have what it takes to become rich.

198. I am thankful for the financial freedom that being wealthy brings.

199. I can bring freedom to myself and to others by generating unlimited amounts of wealth.

200. My family and friends are happy to see me succeed.

201. I can have whatever I want whenever I want it.

202. I seem to be at the right place at the right moment all of the time.

203. There is more money available than any of us can even imagine.

204. I am not just lucky—I deserve all the money I work to generate.

205. I attract more and more money with each passing year.

206. I am so happy to have met and exceeded my financial goals.

207. I am grateful to have more money than I know what to do with. I will use it to provide greater service to humankind.

208. I can be whoever and whatever I want for the rest of my life.

209. I can do whatever I want for the rest of my life.

210. I can have whatever I want for the rest of my life.

211. I am a natural born success.

212. There is no such thing as luck—I earned everything I have.

213. I am destined to be rich.

214. I am destined to be wealthy.

215. I am destined to be successful.

216. Every day that goes by, I get richer and richer.

217. I am a powerful creative force, which is why it is easy for me to create wealth.

218. I share my talents and execute ideas with the world, and receive lots of money in return.

219. I have a clear idea of how much money I want to earn and what I am going to do to earn it.

220. I believe in my ability to make massive amounts of money.

221. I have the ability to create a million dollars over and over again.

222. Wealth is a mindset and I am wealthy inside and out.

223. Wealth outside comes from wealth within, and I have wealth within.

224. Money is a constantly renewing resource for me.

225. I am unified with wealth and prosperity.

226. My money is always multiplying.

227. I transform the lives of others with the money I attract into my life.

228. Money always flows into my life like a rushing river.

229. Wealth and prosperity are my birthright.

230. I was born rich on the inside, so I can easily get rich on the outside.

231. My external wealth is a reflection of my internal wealth.

232. I am willing to make whatever changes or improvements needed in myself to reach my financial goals.

233. It is fun to be rich and enjoy financial freedom.

234. My success breeds more success.

235. My wealth breeds more wealth.

236. My investments continually multiply, bringing me more money than I imagined.

237. I make money in my sleep with the power of my investments.

238. I make money in my sleep with the power of my passive income vehicles.

239. I can manifest millions.

240. I am excited about generating millions of dollars in my life.

241. I love money and money loves me.

242. I am good and money is too.

243. I easily achieve my financial goals.

244. I always knew I would become rich.

245. I love money because money allows me to do what I love.

246. My bank accounts grow constantly without limit.

247. I am living my perfect life.

248. I am rich and confident.

249. I am prosperous and love helping others.

250. All of my businesses are successful.

251. Everything I touch turns to gold.

252. I attract successful people who work in harmony with me.

253. I am growing richer and richer and am able to easily provide for my family.

254. I have enough wealth to take care of my family for the rest of their lives.

255. Because I am rich, I decide what I will do with my time.

256. I have unlimited amounts of wealth and can share it with others and generate even more wealth.

257. My choices are unlimited, and I can help others without limit.

258. I enjoy being a multi-millionaire.

259. I allow myself to feel success and enjoy the fruits of my labor.

260. I feel like a success, I act like a success, I am a success.

261. I have no problems going out and claiming what is mine, and wealth is mine.

262. I expect prosperity and riches to flow to me.

263. I joyously accept the money that flows into my life.

264. Money is only a tool that allows me to live the life of freedom that I want.

265. Success is my new normal.

266. Wealth is my new normal.

267. Abundance is my new normal.

268. I am amazed at how easily unlimited amounts of money come into my life.

269. I am attracted to money the way magnets are attracted to each other.

270. It was always my destiny to become rich.

271. Wealth generating ideas continually flow into my head.

272. Every success I enjoy generates a new success.

273. Every dollar I earn turns into another.

274. Prosperity is my natural state of being.

275. I am a magnet for millions of dollars.

276. I deserve to make millions.

277. Rich people are good people, and I am both.

278. Wealth is nothing more than energy, and I am continually drawing it towards me.

279. I can create a million dollars at will.

280. I am debt free and prosperous.

281. Everything that I need has been provided for me.

282. I can realize all my dreams.

283. Money is not just for others: it is for me.

284. I am confident in my abilities to grow my money resources.

285. I enjoy the rewards I earn from the service I provide to others.

286. Success is all around me.

287. I am both happy and rich.

288. I am at peace with my wealth and my ability to maintain it.

289. I am at peace with my wealth and my ability to grow it.

290. My hard work pays off with financial rewards.

291. Earning money has always been easy for me.

292. Getting rich is a skill of mine.

293. Making money is easy when you provide value to others.

294. I alone am responsible for my relationship with money.

295. I alone am responsible for my attitude toward money.

296. My talents and persistence guarantee my success.

297. Abundance is a natural part of my life.

298. I can always generate the money I need or want.

299. Money is my friend: it will help me to help others.

300. I am highly motivated in the pursuit of my financial goals.

301. I know that I will receive money in proportion to the value I provide others.

302. I do not always have to work for money because my money works for me.

303. I am always attracting prosperous investment opportunities.

304. I am happy that I benefit financially from lucrative investments.

305. I am motivated to do a great job and get my work done on time.

306. I will always earn more than enough money than I need to survive.

307. The value I provide others translates into money I deserve.

308. I have a lot to offer others and will be compensated in direct proportion to what I choose to provide.

309. I am deserving of the wealth I am constantly creating.

310. My talents are a gift to this world, and I deserve the money they generate for me and my family.

311. My unique talents benefit those around me and help us all excel to the best of our abilities.

312. I trust in my ability to generate money and prosperity and I will get it done.

313. I believe in my ability to keep going when things get tough.

314. I trust in my ability to amass wealth regardless of the political climate.

315. I trust in my ability to amass wealth no matter the state of the economy.

316. I bring in wealth from all corners of the world.

317. I am connected to the global economy and have customers all over the globe.

318. I trust myself to make wise and prosperous financial decisions.

319. Money always has and always will come naturally to me.

320. My mind is strong and helps me generate new ideas that attract money.

321. I don't earn money: I attract it in direct proportion to the amount of value that I provide.

322. I refuse to let others place limits on the amount of money that I can attain in my life.

323. There are no limits to the level to which I can monetize my talents.

324. There are no limits to the level to which I can monetize my ideas.

325. My exceptional intuition guides me when it comes to deciding what to do with my money.

326. I have everything required to become a success.

327. Success, wealth, and financial prosperity are natural and my birthright.

328. I am proud of the money I earn because I know I deserve it.

329. I am happy to be rich because I believe I am worth it.

330. I am just as deserving as others are of becoming wealthy and financially free.

331. I am always making money, whether I am actively working or not.

332. I am following the path toward more wealth and riches.

333. I can create any amount of money that anyone can name.

334. I easily learn new skills that help me earn more money.

335. I am intuitively pointed in the direction of wealth.

336. I am grateful to have the money to spend on things that will enrich and improve my life.

337. I am always planting seeds to help me earn more money in the future.

338. I love my work and the financial reward it brings.

339. I take action each and every day that will increase my income.

340. I am grateful to have plenty of money to invest in my own mental health.

341. I am grateful to have plenty of money to invest in my own spiritual health.

342. I am grateful to have plenty of money to invest in my own physical health.

343. I love treating myself and the people I love with the money I have.

344. My wealth is constantly compounding over time.

Chapter 24
Affirmations for Attitude and Relationship with Money

Your attitude toward money has a significant impact on whether or not you attract money into your life. If you grew up in an atmosphere that destroyed your self-esteem and left you lacking in desire and ambition, it will be more difficult for you to attract financial resources.

In addition, if you believe you do not deserve to be rich or that money is corrupt, you are likely to believe that you do not deserve to have sufficient financial resources, even if you consciously wish you had more.

If you have a bad attitude about money, you will not put up the effort necessary to get it. You will not pay attention to opportunities, and you may even make some mistakes in judgment that result in losing money.

With repeatedly repeating affirmations intended to change your attitude toward money, your subconscious mind will ultimately accept them as real, and a negative attitude toward money will gradually be replaced by a good attitude.

The Affirmations

1. It is never a problem for me to have more than enough money to suit my requirements.

2. I pay myself first, but I always share my money to help others who need help.

3. I deserve to be wealthy.

4. My wealth grows in proportion to the service I provide others.

5. My wealth grows in proportion to the value I provide others.

6. I can afford anything and everything my heart desires.

7. I am drawing money toward me all the time.

8. I have the power to create all the wealth my family needs.

9. I deserve financial abundance and material prosperity.

10. I own money, but money does not own me.

11. I find it easy to attract money into my life.

12. I choose to be rich and powerful but will use it to make a positive impact in the lives of others.

13. I know that my wealth is not just for me but for the betterment of others as well.

14. The world is full of riches, and I know that I will get my share.

15. I attract money wherever I go - no matter what I am doing.

16. I love money and feel the good that comes from it.

17. I am the one who has complete control over the amount of money I have in my life.

18. I choose to be wealthy and recognize that life is magnificent.

19. Money is good when it is used for good.

20. I am increasing my wealth, which gives me the power to increase my freedom.

21. I use money to open new doors to more success.

22. Money is a tool that I can use to create my best life.

23. Money is a tool that I can use to support others in living their best life.

24. Having or wanting money is nothing to feel guilt or shame over.

25. Money is a seed, which when planted properly, will grow.

26. I freely invest money into my business, knowing that I will always make a significant return.

27. I freely invest money into myself, knowing that I will always make a significant return.

28. I am responsible with my money, and I always find ways to make it grow.

29. I use and invest my money responsibly.

30. I enjoy the power that comes from financial independence.

31. I am always growing my wealth, no matter the state of the economy.

32. I am always growing my wealth, no matter the political climate.

33. I act on my ideas that create prosperity.

34. My wealth is growing every single day.

35. I am just as capable of creating, growing, and maintaining wealth as anyone else.

36. It is possible for money to come and flow to me easily.

37. I choose to share my wealth with others.

38. I find it easy to make money and make more and more with each passing day.

39. I attract wealth to me from all corners of the world.

40. I am strong enough to grow wealth despite my upbringing.

41. I have a positive mental attitude around money.

42. I have a healthy relationship with money.

43. I am in control of money, not the other way around.

44. I am unstoppable when it comes to generating massive wealth.

45. I enjoy making money.

46. My income is always effortlessly increasing.

47. I don't always have to work for money, I make my money work for me.

48. I put my money to work in profitable investments.

49. I make passive income from my money.

50. While I sleep and play, my money is still working and growing for me.

51. I can make lots of money without trading my time for it.

52. The actions I do today will result in more wealth, prosperity, and abundance.

53. I feel good, joyous, and positive when it comes to money.

54. Money is not the only thing that brings me happiness and fulfilment.

55. It is okay to feel happy and excited about making money.

56. It is okay to be wealthy.

57. It is my right to be rich.

58. My bank account continues to grow more than I ever thought possible.

59. I use the money I have to make more money.

60. I have all the wealth I could ever need or want.

61. I am surrounded by wealth and abundance.

62. My relationships are just as rich as my bank account.

63. I am always receiving wealth because I am willing to ask for it.

64. I am always receiving wealth because I am willing to work for it.

65. My inputs result in increase.

66. Having money gives me options, which is a good thing.

67. Wealth allows me to choose what I want for my life, while poverty would make my choices for me.

68. I have the ability to attract money and wealth to myself.

69. I have so much wealth I can share it with others effortlessly.

70. I can create and produce whatever amount of money I need at will.

71. I have the money I want and need because I ask for the money I want and need.

72. I am surrounded by opportunities to make more money.

73. I already have the ideas I need to make more money, I just need to act on them.

74. The world has all the money I could ever want.

75. I earn my money, fair and square.

76. I can make a lot of money and still be a good person.

77. I have my own positive opinions of money despite the opinions of others from my past.

78. I have my own positive relationship to money despite others from my past.

79. I can be both rich and humble.

80. I can be both rich and kind.

81. I can be both rich and loving.

82. I can be both rich and generous.

83. I can be both rich and honest.

84. I provide value and service to others in my work, which results in more money and wealth for me.

85. I have the capability to be responsible with my wealth.

86. I have the capability to grow my wealth.

87. As my professional service and contribution grow, as does my bank account.

88. I never take more in monetary value from others than value I provide them.

89. I deserve the wealth that I am receiving.

90. Whether it take a short or a long time to grow my wealth, I am as patient as I need to be.

91. Money is drawn to me and I accept it with gratitude.

92. I respect money and recognize it as a tool that provides liberty, prosperity, and freedom.

93. Money gives me opportunities in life to do, have, and become things that most can only dream of.

94. I enjoy money, wealth, and prosperity.

95. I am comfortable with having wealth and riches.

96. I deserve financial independence and financial abundance.

97. If I wish to raise my income, I must also raise my living standards, as well.

98. In order for my money to grow, I must grow.

99. I am always able to figure out ways to make money.

100. I am free of debt.

101. Anything I want, I can pay for in full.

102. I surround myself with people who are financially responsible.

103. I have an abundance of money that can help me handle any life situation that comes up.

104. I am master over my money, not the other way around.

105. I will always be wealthy.

106. Everyone deserves to have money to live their best life, and I will take my share without guilt.

107. I see a way to make money from new ideas every day.

108. I am comfortable with the money that hard work brings.

109. I have so much money that I always feel financially secure.

110. Money is good because it brings security to my family.

111. Money is good: it makes it easier for me to help others.

112. My mind is clear and calm because my financial needs are taken care of.

113. Money provides me with the opportunity to accomplish what I want, rather than merely what I am required to do.

114. Money is a ticket that allows me to do whatever I want in life.

115. Being wealthy allows me to make decisions based on growth and desire, not desperation and restriction.

116. What I earn has absolutely nothing to do with how well the economy is doing right now.

117. I thrive in economic times where others panic.

118. There are opportunities all around me to grow wealth.

119. Money is generously given to me and I generously give it to others.

120. I trust that I will always have more than enough money to meet my needs.

121. I love the feeling I get when I receive money well-earned.

122. I am thankful and appreciative when I receive money because I know that others don't always have it.

123. I find it easy to meet my financial goals.

124. My financial security makes it possible to help others.

125. My money allows me to better support my health.

126. Every single day, the amount of money I have grows.

127. I feel light and happy when I think about money.

128. The thing I love the most about money is how it enables me to change the world.

129. The stronger I am the more money I attract.

130. I deserve any amount of money I could wish for.

131. I have all the money I could possibly dream of.

132. I am proud and deserving of the wealth and money I have earned.

133. My wealthy mindset enables me to create money.

134. I admire the wealthy and successful and strive to be more like them.

135. I learn from rich and successful people who teach me about wealth generation.

136. My heart is open to receiving wealth, money, and prosperity.

137. I am getting closer and closer to my financial goals every day.

138. I allow and welcome wealth and money to enter into my life.

139. Financial increase is constant and inevitable for me.

140. I am comfortable looking at my bank account and seeing it grow.

141. I can earn as much money as I want and need.

142. Being wealthy and prosperous is my natural state of being.

143. I set financial goals and always achieve them faster than I thought I would.

144. Money can help buy happiness because it buys opportunity and freedom of choice.

145. I give myself permission to be rich.

146. It's okay for me to maximize my potential by making as much money as I possibly can.

147. I do the world a favor by making as much money as I possibly can.

148. I do my loved ones a favor by making as much money as I possibly can.

149. I do myself a favor by making as much money as I possibly can.

150. It goes without saying that the more money I earn, the more money I can contribute.

151. The more money I earn, the more money I am able to give away.

152. My ability to grow wealth is inspiring to others.

153. Pursuing wealth makes me a better person because I have to grow as a person for my money to grow.

154. Money is good and helps others.

155. I am responsible with my money, but I also enjoy it.

156. I gladly allow wealth to enter my life.

157. I can and will become rich, solely because I choose to.

158. I spend money without guilt or shame.

159. I love spending money on others to help them get what they need and desire.

160. I deserve all the money I have and even more.

161. I deserve all the money that is coming to me, and even more.

162. I give myself permission to openly receive all the money that is coming to me.

163. I feel good about money and enjoy it.

164. My heart is completely open to abundance and prosperity.

165. Money flows into my life without me asking for it because I am a magnet for money.

166. I am grateful for the money that keeps flowing into my life and I will use it for good.

167. I effortlessly attract money into my life through the service that I provide others.

168. I earn my money and my wealth because I make myself a valuable asset to the world.

169. I enjoy investing and love using my money to grow more money.

170. I take calculated financial risks because I am confident I can make them pay off.

171. In my professional life, I fulfill the needs of others in a moral way, and receive money in return.

172. The abundance I have makes me feel light and stress free.

173. I believe I have the ability to earn as much money as I desire.

174. I am mentally strong, so I can earn money in any way that I set out to.

175. I am resourceful, so I can earn money in any way that I set out to.

176. Every single day, I wake up with more money than I had the day before.

177. Every day, my income and my professional success are growing.

178. Attaining financial prosperity is my right and responsibility.

179. It is easy for me to manifest wealth.

180. I help others get the money they desire and deserve because there is plenty for everyone to succeed.

181. I admire honest, wealthy people and value the positive example they provide.

182. I learn from others how to increase my own wealth.

183. I am financially rewarded in proportion to the quality of work I do.

184. My mind and conscience are at ease when I spend money.

185. My mind and conscience are at ease when I grow money.

186. I can boldly say that I love making money.

187. I can boldly say that I love having money.

188. I can boldly say that I love spending money.

189. I can boldly say that I love saving money.

190. I can boldly say that I love growing money.

191. I am comfortable with spending and enjoying my money because I know more is always coming my way.

192. Money is a resource that is always renewing for me.

193. It is okay for me to spend money on the things I want.

194. It is okay for me to spend money on others.

195. I save and invest out of responsibility not fear because I know more is always coming to me.

196. I always exceed my financial goals and make more money than I want.

197. I grow wealth in every type of economic or political climate.

198. The world is full of money-making opportunities and I always seize them.

199. I can afford to spend lots of money on personal care because of my wealth.

200. I use my money to create the best life for myself and others.

201. Generating wealth is on auto pilot for me.

202. I love money and wealth.

203. I celebrate being able to buy a wonderful home for myself and my family.

204. I enjoy my financial blessings.

205. I use money to learn more and educate myself, to increase my value to others.

206. I have more than enough money and share my overflow with others.

207. I am a positive example for others to embrace money and the freedom it provides.

208. I love to give money away because I can easily create more.

209. I could regenerate my wealth from scratch if I had to.

210. I have a wealth mindset and have a positive attitude about money.

211. I find it easy to make money on demand.

212. The ability to help others motivates me to grow my wealth even more.

213. I am rich, wealth, and prosperous.

214. My investments always yield long term profits.

215. I am growing richer by the day.

216. I am skilled in creating and generating money.

217. I can create money-making opportunities for myself and for others.

218. I share money making opportunities with others because there is more than enough money to go around.

219. I am always discovering new money-making opportunities.

220. I have the power to generate my own money, regardless of what is going on in my environment.

221. It is okay for money to make me feel happy.

222. My subconscious acts in alignment with my conscious efforts to earn and grow wealth.

223. I have the power to create money through my mind and can do so whenever I need to.

224. I have the power to attract money into my life and increase prosperity.

225. I have the power to forever defeat debt and poverty.

226. I feel joy and satisfaction when I have the money to spend on things I want and need.

227. Wealth is the natural state of my life.

228. Having lots of money is the natural state of my life.

229. With every new day, I will claim the money-making opportunities it brings.

230. I choose to feel good about money, and the prosperity and security it can bring.

231. I choose to feel good about money, and the mental peace it can bring.

232. I love all the money I earn and every dollar in my bank account.

233. I cultivate positive feelings about money every day.

234. Money supports my life and dreams in every possible way.

235. I choose to let go of the negative feelings I have about money and wealth.

236. I choose to let go of the negative perceptions I have about money that I got from other people.

237. I use my leadership abilities and intelligence to attract money.

238. To receive money in the future, I will render services to others while expecting nothing in return.

239. I use seed money to plant new riches to be realized in the future.

240. I donate to worthy causes out of the goodness of my heart.

241. I feel myself becoming more and more wealthy each passing day.

242. Pursing financial goals is a worthy pursuit.

243. I make sound financial decisions.

244. I have gratitude for all the wealth and money I have received, created, and built.

245. I make lots of money and deserve every dollar of it.

246. I give away money every month to help realize other people's dreams and make the world a better place

Chapter 25
Affirmations for Handling Professional, Work, and Business Stress

Just as you can't stop mistakes from occurring, you can't also stop people from criticizing you. Like mistakes, criticism will influence your self-esteem only if you let them. Don't allow criticism to make you forget your self-esteem or core values.

To prevent criticism from having a damaging impact on your self-esteem, you have to learn how to cope with it. This segment will teach you how to respond to critics in an effective manner. But before that, there are a number of things you should understand about reality:

1. **People are different:** they see things differently, have different tastes, beliefs, behavior patterns and psychological makeup. You shouldn't regard their critical statements as the complete truth. For instance, someone who is naturally outgoing won't understand why you don't mingle with people. The person will immediately criticize you for being boring or too shy because he/she is unable to understand that your introversion is okay.

2. **Emotions color people's perceptions:** When people are feeling a certain way, their emotions color their words or actions. Your girlfriend may have called you wasteful for using up the remaining supplies because she just got fired and is feeling paranoid. If you start going over his criticism in your head and believing that you lack judgment, your self-esteem suffers for something that is not even the truth.

In conclusion, before you accept any critical remark as the ultimate truth about yourself, first reflect on the critic's overall makeup. And when responding to criticism, be neither passive nor aggressive; rather acknowledge the criticism by telling the person that they are right and provide an explanation if necessary. That is the only way to stop criticism instantly.

The Affirmations

1. I am doing my best at work and that is the best that I can do.
2. I am a valuable asset to any professional team.
3. I can get through any project if I just take things one step at a time.
4. The only thing I focus on is the task in front of me right now.
5. I am productive and focused and I easily check things off my to-do list.
6. I have more than enough time to accomplish the things I need to accomplish.
7. I will find my ideal career and make it mine.
8. I will create my ideal business if that is my desire.
9. My income is always increasing from the work that I do.
10. I radiate energy and confidence when I am at work.
11. My career does not take over my life.
12. Other areas of my life are just as important as the way I make money.
13. I am grateful to have found and realized my professional dreams.

14. The contacts that I need to help me advance professionally are on their way to me.

15. I attract positive mentors who guide me towards success in my chosen field.

16. I am grateful to have a lucrative source of income that supports my dream lifestyle.

17. I am always finding opportunities to grow and expand in my career.

18. I know I will always excel no matter what I do.

19. I am recognized for the quality work I contribute to my field.

20. Even better opportunities are always just around the corner.

21. I am in control of my professional path.

22. I will shape my career to be the way I want it to be.

23. I make great professional connections because I am confident in my abilities.

24. If I decide to change my career, it will lead me to something bigger and better.

25. I am fulfilled by my work.

26. I am challenged by my work in a positive and productive way.

27. I get excited to get to go to work each day.

28. I lead my team with humility and grace.

29. My career helps me grow into becoming a better person.

30. There is a successful business owner inside me who can manage a business to perfection.

31. I will find my way to the top of any field.

32. I am able to learn the skills I may need to learn to get the job done.

33. I bring excellence to every task, no matter how big or small.

34. I am calmly confident in my ability to manage my business and make it highly successful.

35. Today is the day that opportunity will knock, and I will open the door.

36. I perform my work with integrity no matter what.

37. I perform my work with pride no matter what.

38. I perform my work with excellence no matter what.

39. I am wealthy because of the dedicated efforts I have put in.

40. I get closer and closer to my business goals every day.

41. I am successful in my career because I take action.

42. I do what it takes to turn my ideas into reality.

43. I am constantly growing my business and professional income.

44. All of my career success just breeds more success.

45. I have a strong network of contacts and am well-regarded in my profession.

46. I always attract positive thinking people to work with me.

47. I always attract hard working people to work with me.

48. I am always learning new ways to do my work faster and better.

49. My professional efficiency increases every day.

50. I have the ability to be the best in whichever profession I choose.

51. I consciously release any and all negative thoughts that will impede my success.

52. I believe in myself and what I am capable of doing.

53. New opportunities are waiting for me and I am ready to grab them.

54. My communication abilities are continuously being refined, and I am continually striving for improvement.

55. Today is going to be a great day at work and every tomorrow will be too.

56. I am my own best motivator.

57. I capitalize on my opportunities by taking action.

58. I will explore all new avenues to success whenever they present themselves.

59. Each new idea is a gift and I will treat it as such.

60. Every day, I will look for new opportunities for further success.

61. Whenever I need assistance, I can attract the best resources possible to fit my needs.

62. Whenever I need assistance, I can attract the best people possible to fit my needs.

63. Whenever I need assistance, I can attract the best solutions possible to fit my needs.

64. I am proficient at time management, which allows me to attain my objectives.

65. I am effective at organization, which helps me achieve my goals.

66. I always find a way to enjoy my work.

67. I am grateful to have a means of making great money.

68. I make sure that my values and ambitions work with each other, not against each other.

69. My work surrounds me with inspiring people who push me to do better.

70. I am grateful to work with people who share in my enthusiasm for the work we do.

71. I welcome new work challenges with calm confidence.

72. I am naturally good at finding solutions to problems.

73. I surround myself with people who are highly successful and who encourage me to be the same.

74. I see a new chance for success in every new challenge I face.

75. Overcoming challenges is a way to improve my self-esteem and self-confidence.

76. When obstacles show up, it's a chance for me to show people what I'm made of.

77. I always take time to celebrate my successes and victories.

78. I trust my intuition to help me make wise professional decisions.

79. I am always in tune and intuitively know the best next step to take.

80. Today will bring an abundance of new ideas that I will use to my advantage.

81. I consistently expect winning solutions, and I always attract good outcomes.

82. I am happy with my growth in my career and expect more to come in the future.

83. I deserve and demand respect in my career.

84. My career path is the best one for me, no matter what other people are doing.

85. I am steadily climbing the ranks in my field.

86. By being myself, I bring something unique and wonderful to my work.

87. I am a successful person by nature.

88. I will remain consistent in my efforts, and will therefore achieve the results I want.

89. I achieve the goals I set out to achieve.

90. I am ambitious by nature.

91. I have a knack for succeeding at everything I do.

92. I am doing my best at work and that is good enough.

93. I keep my dreams alive with my positive attitude.

94. I always go the extra mile, and it always pays off.

95. I know that my dedication will lead to promotion and increase.

96. I have the energy of a winner because I am a winner.

97. I have the energy of a success because I am a success.

98. I bring joy and light into my workplace with my positive attitude and winning smile.

99. I only speak positively about those that I work with.

100. I have healthy, fulfilling, positive relationships with the people I work with.

101. I speak up boldly and ask intelligent questions when needed.

102. I create my own opportunities and don't just wait for them to come to me.

103. My repertoire of skills is constantly expanding.

104. I put consistent effort and energy into becoming better at what I do.

105. People take notice of my skill and work ethic.

106. I appreciate everyone, both above and below me, who helps contribute to my success.

107. I get what I want in my work by helping other people get what they want.

108. I keep my workspace clean so my mind will be clean.

109. I keep my workspace organized so my mind will be organized.

110. I always see the fruits of my labor.

111. Seeing other people ahead of me simply drives me to be better.

112. I always persist and never quit because things get too hard.

113. I have the wisdom to know when to try a different tactic.

114. I am especially gifted at what I do.

115. I will maintain a positive outlook at work today no matter what happens.

116. Communication with those that I work with is something I do very well.

117. I am only finished with a project when I know it is the best I could have done.

118. The work I do is always done to the best of my ability.

119. I only turn in quality projects, done with care.

120. I set a great example for other people in my field.

121. I'm always learning, so I can stay relevant in my field.

122. I have the power to make today a good day or a bad day and I choose to have a good day at work today.

123. All of the work that I do is important and significant.

124. I radiate confidence in my abilities, which gets me noticed.

125. I am open to doing whatever it takes to get the job done.

126. I deserve to be financially stable and I will do what I need to do to get there.

127. I always have the best team to work with.

128. I work with a team of people with unique and valuable skills.

129. I always bring the best out of the people I work with.

130. I am trusted in my field as an honest leader.

Chapter 26
Affirmations for Protecting and Improving Your Mental State and Confidence

Your influence, dear black man, has the power to transform the world. You've influenced generations. You've commanded armies. You've governed whole countries. Presidents, billionaires, physicians, attorneys, accountants, entrepreneurs, tradespeople, farmers, dads, brothers, and cousins are among the people you've become. Examine your local environment and seek to improve yourself and the people around you. Look for ways to improve your financial literacy and gain economic power. As powerful as an ocean current and as furious and relentless as the wind, be a positive, inspiring force. You, black guy, are a game-changer. Face the challenge.

To start believing your realistic self-description, write a new description of yourself that you will read out to yourself every day for a month till it drowns out the voice of that vicious inner critic you've been listening to for years. The new description should incorporate the tips outlined above: no use of pejoratives, generalization, exaggeration, or vagueness.

Make sure you defend yourself with positive affirmations of your strength whenever your critic starts bombarding you with negativity. Sure, the critic can be cunny and relentless, attacking you with memories or thoughts that are hard to ignore, making your attempts at accurate thinking useless. Let the rebuttal voice of your accepting friend, rational teacher, healthy coach, or compassionate mentor do the talking.

But you can still emerge a victor in this war against the critic. Distancing yourself from your mind or thoughts is another weapon you can add to the special arsenal you have for fighting the critic.

The Affirmations

1. Things don't have to be flawless in order to be successful.
2. I work calmly because I know things will ultimately work out.
3. I believe that everything will work out as it should.
4. I only use my own measurements for success, not someone else's.
5. Based on my personal definition of success, I know I am on the right path for myself.
6. When something difficult comes my way, I am entirely capable of navigating my way through it.
7. The answers I am seeking are already inside me.
8. Every issue has a solution, and I will be the one to uncover it.
9. My thoughts are centered, and my will is strong.
10. I always remain mentally calm despite what's going on around me.
11. I am impervious to drama and negativity because I have the emotional intelligence to not take anything personally.
12. I have the power to calm my mind and put myself at ease at any time.
13. I work towards my goals with relaxation and ease.

14. I have peace in knowing that I have an instinct that guides me towards success.

15. Contentment and calmness come naturally to me.

16. Mental peace and clarity come naturally to me.

17. Ideas and solutions come naturally to me.

18. I relinquish the concept that I must bear the full weight of things on my shoulders.

19. I reframe failure as a positive thing that is necessary for success.

20. Failure is really just a lesson on how to do better next time.

21. I do not over-inflate problems to be bigger than they are.

22. My calmness puts people around me at ease.

23. I attract other people who are also mentally calm.

24. I love moments of solitude as opportunities to mentally reset.

25. I love moments of solitude as opportunities to calm my mind.

26. I love moments of solitude as opportunities to replenish my spirit.

27. I am unapologetic with taking and protecting my alone time.

28. I am more than good enough for the rewards that come from my dedication.

29. I am fully deserving of reaping the benefits of the fruits of my labor.

30. I take the steps necessary to maintain a good energy field around myself.

31. In this moment, everything is okay.

32. I easily get into flow states of unstoppable creativity.

33. Getting in the zone mentally is easy for me.

34. I know how to channel myself into any attitude necessary for the task at hand.

35. I have the ability to clear my mind on command.

36. I have complete control over my thoughts.

37. I take full responsibility for my thoughts.

38. I have complete control over my emotions.

39. I take full responsibility for my emotions.

40. I have complete control over my reactions.

41. I take full responsibility for my reactions.

42. I only utilize my mental energy for what is in front of me right now.

43. I tackle things one thing at a time to avoid overwhelm.

44. Mental stillness and meditation are a frequent practice of mine.

45. I have the power to find peace within myself.

46. In times of turmoil, I go back to my breath to regain my calm.

47. I feel at peace with everything in my life.

48. I am completely and fully in the present moment.

49. Failure is beneficial because it teaches me what not to do in the future.

50. I live and operate only in the now.

51. When the time comes, the future will take care of itself and will also take care of me, if I let it.

52. I do not have to identify with every thought that comes through my head.

53. I do not have to believe every thought that comes through my head.

54. I do not have to succumb emotionally to every thought that comes through my head.

55. I choose to only believe things that are helpful and beneficial to me in some way.

56. I have the power to just let a thought pass by if it does not serve me.

57. My mind is kind to me and shows me that I am deserving of peace.

58. Tranquility is my natural state.

59. My mental peace is my priority.

60. I am emotionally strong and mentally fit.

61. I can find a complete state of serenity at will whenever needed.

62. Even when there is chaos around me, I am calm and tranquil within me.

63. Throughout the day, my subconscious mind is always working in my favor.

64. Though I strive for more, I am content with what I have.

65. I am patient and willing to wait for my greatest blessings to unfold in their due time.

66. If I put in the work, I know I will reap the reward.

67. I welcome failure and all the lessons it brings.

68. Whenever I think of all the things I'm grateful for, I immediately feel better.

69. I have a habitual practice of gratitude.

70. I am capable of making choices that will bring more goodness into my life.

71. I am working to become better, but I am happy about who I am.

72. When new issues arise, I remain calm and focused as the solution finds its way to me.

73. Each failure just gets me closer to a success.

74. I am capable of learning whatever I need to learn to do whatever I need to do.

75. There is no success without failure.

76. I am mentally strong enough to work through distractions that would normally derail others.

77. I am mentally strong enough to work through obstacles that would normally derail others.

78. I am mentally strong enough to overcome failures that would normally derail others.

79. I do what needs to be done immediately so I can keep my mental space clear.

80. My mind is my greatest tool, so I protect it fiercely.

81. My peace is my greatest asset, so I protect it fiercely.

82. I can activate my concentration on command.

83. My concentration skills are getting better each day.

84. I consciously engage only in healthy thought patterns.

85. I keep my body in top condition so I can keep my mind in top condition.

86. I take breaks without guilt, and always return to my task with renewed focus and energy.

87. I can quickly refocus myself when my mind wanders.

88. Momentary failure does not exempt me from ultimate success.

89. My mind stays clear because I do what I know I should do when I know I should do it.

90. I am able to separate myself from my constant inner monologue.

91. I am ruler over the background noise in my head.

92. I control my thoughts, my thoughts do not control me.

93. I conduct myself thoughtfully and consciously.

94. My healthy lifestyle empowers me by giving me the physical and mental energy I need.

95. In times of big decisions, I am patient with myself as I determine the best way to move forward.

96. I know I do my best, which is the only validation I need.

97. It is more important for something to be complete than be perfect.

98. I act with consideration but without hesitation because I trust my instincts.

99. I feel happier and more positive when I take initiative and take action.

100. I am able to put my head down and work on the process, and let the result work itself out.

101. I can call on my focus at will to gain momentum on whatever I need to do.

102. My mind is sharp and alert.

103. My mind is present and focused on the task at hand.

104. When my environment is decluttered, so is my head.

105. I love the feeling of making something complete over making something perfect.

106. When I focus on the present moment, I feel calm and ready to take on anything.

107. I am motivated and excited, yet relaxed in all that I do.

108. Whatever I put my focus on expands, so I choose where I put my focus wisely.

109. A better body means a better mind, so I am diligent in taking care of my body.

110. I feed healthy foods to my body and healthy thoughts to my brain.

111. The more I push myself mentally, the stronger I become.

112. The stronger mentally that I become, the easier it is for me to do what I need to do.

113. I am capable of pushing past my perceived limits.

114. I am so excited to meet the version of myself that lives on the other side of my current mental barriers.

115. My mind is better because of the respect that I show my body.

116. I am disciplined in my self-care because I know how great it makes me feel and perform.

117. I am empathetic with myself when I have a bad day.

118. I do not perform at the same level every day, but I do my best every day, and that is good enough for me.

119. Because I am active, my brain is active.

120. A healthy body equals a healthy mind.

121. I can put aside tomorrow's cares in order to focus on today's tasks.

122. My mental clarity allows me to make wise decisions for my work and personal life.

123. I have the mental wherewithal to do what I said I was going to do whether I feel like it or not.

124. Excuses don't stop me from doing what I know I need to do.

125. I take action based on my commitments, not my feelings.

126. I follow through on what I say. I'm going to do what I say I'm going to do when I say I'm going to do it.

127. I have confidence in my abilities because I know I can count on myself to do what I say I'll do.

128. I take care of my environment and workspace to promote a better state of mental well-being.

129. The state of my physical space is a reflection of the state of my mental space.

130. I only own things that make my life easier and happier.

131. I fully trust those that I delegate tasks to, relieving myself of mental load.

132. Everything does not have to go exactly according to my plan.

133. My only focus is meeting my expectations of myself, not the expectations others have of me.

134. I am in tune to when I need to make a shift or change in my life.

135. I trust my intuition and my gut feelings.

136. I settle my nerves by following my instincts.

137. My body carries my mind, and for that, I treat it well.

138. My emotional and mental well-being are supported by my physical health and nutrition.

139. I know when it is best to let go rather than try to control every person and situation around me.

140. I take care of my space as a means of taking care of my mind.

141. When I clean up the mess in my space, I clean up the mess in my head.

142. Every day will not be a great and perfect day, and that is okay.

143. It's never too late for me to get back on track.

144. I can easily make up for what feels like lost time in the pursuit of my goals.

145. If I keep moving forward, I will arrive at my goal destination right on time.

146. I do what I need to do to keep my spirits up and my mood high.

147. Despite the fact that I am not perfect, I am still amazing.

148. I accept myself fully for all my imperfections.

149. My clean and clear environment make for a clean and clear mind.

150. I dedicate time to relaxing as well as working.

151. My relationships and hobbies are just as important as my professional contributions to the world.

152. I always allow myself a mental reset before going back into another taxing project.

153. A healthy diet and exercise regimen keep me focused and clear-headed.

154. Everything will be okay if something does not go completely as planned.

155. My perception of my own actions is in my control.

156. All good things take time, and I am willing to wait, while taking action.

157. I am in a process and will respect that process.

158. I cannot control how everything will turn out, but I can control how it will control me.

Chapter 27
Affirmations for Gratitude

One of the most beneficial personal development exercises you may engage in is the practice of daily gratitude affirmations, which can be done at any time of day. You will experience pleasure, happiness, and tranquility in your life if you are grateful. It also actually assists you in achieving your objectives and fulfilling your aspirations.

Positive affirmations rewire your brain to think in a more productive way. When you combine positive affirmations with appreciation, you have superpowers for manifesting your dreams and desires in your life.

Gratitude is the most ever powerful human emotion, and it has the ability to improve your attitude, health, and whole life experience. A regular practice of gratitude affirmations may have a profound impact on your overall well-being on several levels, also including the physical, mental or emotional, and energy.

As a result, your energy vibration, mood, hormone levels, and overall health are all impacted negatively. Maintaining a good attitude not only makes life simpler and more enjoyable, but it also has a favorable impact on your physical health.

Your body actually secretes stress hormones such as cortisol and adrenaline when you are worried, furious, terrified, or apprehensive in order to assist you in dealing with the perceived threat by either fleeing or combating it.

The fight-or-flight reaction, which has been around for thousands of years, is still present in people today. The trouble is that if you are always worried or nervous, a little quantity of these hormones is being released into your bloodstream on a continuous basis, which is harmful.

These hormones cause inflammation, which in turn contributes to a slew of chronic health disorders.

Chronic stress also slows your metabolism, makes it difficult to lose weight, prevents you from getting enough sleep, and creates brain fog, exhaustion, and a lack of enthusiasm. Cultivating a regular practice of thankfulness affirmations may help to reduce the stress response in the body. As a consequence, you will feel more energized, healthier, lighter, well-rested, and encouraged to continue working toward your objectives.

The Affirmations

1. I keep an inventory of things I am grateful for every single day.

2. My happiness and mental state are improved because I express gratitude regularly.

3. I am grateful to have family and friends in my life who love and support me.

4. I am thankful that expressing gratitude allows me to tap into a well of positive emotions.

5. I appreciate that gratitude and love can boost my self-worth and self-confidence.

6. I am grateful for the level of education and wisdom that I have attained thus far.

7. I appreciate the ability gratitude has to strengthen my personal relationships.

8. I am fortunate to have gratitude, because it gives me a brighter, more optimistic outlook.

9. I am grateful for the chance to make a positive difference in the lives of others in both big and small ways.

10. I appreciate that I have the opportunity to work hard and improve the lives of others.

11. I am grateful for my health and a sound mind.

12. I am fortunate to have family and friends who are there for me when I need help and support.

13. I appreciate my insatiable curiosity and childlike wonder for life.

14. I am grateful to see life in a way that is always interesting and enjoyable.

15. I enjoy every bit of my life's journey, and appreciate even the small moments of joy it brings.

16. I am happy to have the freedom to make my own choices.

17. I am glad that I am always in control of the direction of my life.

18. I am grateful to be the unique combination of external and internal traits that make me, me.

19. I am grateful for the warmth and life giving powers of the sun.

20. I am grateful for the natural processes of nature that make the world run smoothly.

21. I am grateful that nature provides all the resources that I need to survive.

22. I am grateful for the planet that I live on and the natural gifts it provides.

23. I am grateful to have empathy and compassion for the predicaments of others.

24. I am grateful to be able to relate to the feelings of others, as it makes my human connections stronger.

25. I am grateful that no matter how much or how little I have, I always have something to give or help others with.

26. I am glad for the chance to spend time with folks that make me feel good about myself and my life.

27. I appreciate the generosity of my family, friends, and partner that enhance my life.

28. the immense gratitude I feel makes me humble, and makes me appreciate everything I have.

29. I am fortunate to have a good sense of humor that helps brighten my days.

30. I am fortunate to have a happy disposition that helps brighten the lives of those around me.

31. I am grateful for the connectedness of the world and the opportunity to travel to enjoy different cultures and experiences.

32. Internet access and the infinite, easy source of information it gives are two things for which I am thankful.

33. I am fortunate to be in an era in which knowledge is freely accessible at the touch of a button on a computer or mobile device.

34. I am grateful to have personal freedom to express myself the way I want.

35. I am grateful expressing my gratitude improves my health and emotional well-being.

36. I am thankful for all my personal teachers who have shown up along the way and made a positive difference in my life.

37. I appreciate that feeling gratitude reduces stress and anxiety.

38. I am grateful for the opportunity to nurture my existing relationships.

39. I am thankful for the diversity and beauty in nature.

40. I always consider myself lucky to have been the recipient of generosity from others.

41. I am grateful that you don't need a lot of money to be happy.

42. I am thankful that the best things in life are free.

43. Feelings of gratitude create feelings of happiness, and happiness leads to success.

44. I am grateful that this world is filled with beauty that costs me nothing to experience and enjoy.

45. I am grateful that sunshine always follows every storm.

46. I appreciate the opportunity to experience things I already love, and also discover new things.

47. I am thankful for the simple moments I can share with the special people in my life.

48. I am grateful for the time I have to spend with the loved ones who matter most.

49. I am fortunate to have honest and loyal, close friends and family.

50. I feel grateful for all the experiences that bring me lasting moments of joy.

51. I appreciate the selflessness of people who work in service jobs that enhance my quality of life.

52. I appreciate the people who don't even know me who work every day to keep me safe.

53. I appreciate the selflessness of everyday heroes who sacrifice their own personal freedom in order to protect mine.

54. I am thankful for all the positive memories I have accumulated over my lifetime of experiences.

55. I am grateful for positive memories that help me vividly and joyously remember loved ones even after they are gone.

56. I am grateful that there is always something amazing to look forward to in my life.

57. I feel grateful for my strength and ability to overcome adversity.

58. I am grateful for the power to forgive and for the forgiveness of others.

59. I appreciate the parents, guardians, and mentors that have instilled positive values in me.

60. I am grateful for the parental figures in my life who have looked out for my best interest and ensured that I was on the right path.

61. I am thankful for the free opportunity every day to experience beautiful sunrises and sunsets.

62. I am grateful that even if I do not have a lot of money that I can always give of my time to make someone else's life better.

63. I appreciate the guidance and wisdom dispensed to me by my family and my mentors.

64. I am blessed to have folks in my life who are willing to provide a hand when I need it.

65. I feel grateful for the feelings of benevolence that motivate me to do good things for others.

66. I appreciate artists who dedicate their lives to sharing their talents by creating images, music, and media that I can enjoy.

67. I am thankful for the relaxing sounds of nature that I can experience any time for free just by going outside.

68. I appreciate the healing power of music and how easily accessible it is.

69. I am grateful to have easy access to information and documentaries that open my mind.

70. I am grateful for being surrounded by new ways of looking at things.

71. I am fortunate to have the ability to communicate my feelings and concerns with others.

72. I am grateful for the ability to spend quality time with the people I love.

73. I am thankful to be able to support my health with both modern and natural medicine.

74. I appreciate all weather because I know that all seasons serve a purpose.

75. I am grateful for pets and animals, and their ability to instantly cultivate feelings of joy and love.

76. I am fortunate to feel hopeful for a brighter future.

77. I am thankful for the holidays that bring my family and friends together.

78. I appreciate all the gifts I have received throughout the years from thoughtful people.

79. I appreciate the sensation of a warm shower on a cold morning.

80. I am grateful for a warm jacket on a winter night.

81. I am grateful for a warm cup of tea on a cold evening.

82. I am grateful for a cool shower on a hot day.

83. I am grateful to have power and control over my mind.

84. I am thankful to have my mental health and emotional well-being.

85. I am grateful for the power and ability I have to set goals and achieve them.

86. I am thankful for the strength and resilience to carry on after temporary setbacks.

87. I am fortunate to have shelter and to have a roof over my head.

88. I am grateful to have access to transportation and the ability to get around to where I need to go.

89. I appreciate the true heroes out there who put their lives at risk to save others.

90. I feel grateful for the simple pleasures in life like fresh new flowers blooming in spring.

91. I like the shifting of the seasons, as well as the explosion of vibrant color that occurs in the autumn.

92. I am fortunate to be alive, and I make the most of every single day I am given.

93. I appreciate moments of solitude that bring me inner peace.

94. I appreciate moments of communion with others who bring me happiness.

95. In gratitude for the chance to learn from my mistakes, I express my gratitude to you.

96. I am thankful for those who use their beautiful words to inspire me and others.

97. I am grateful for the endless career possibilities that I have.

98. I feel fortunate to have loved ones who know just what to say or do to cheer me up.

99. I am grateful that there are those who are concerned enough to inquire about my well-being.

100. I am grateful for all the hobbies and interests that I am passionate about.

101. I am thankful for all of the successes I have had so far in my life.

102. I feel fortunate for all the happy moments I have to cherish.

103. I feel grateful that positive thinking is always a choice available to me.

104. I am grateful for the days when I am able to disconnect and decompress.

105. I am grateful that after the winter, spring always returns, bringing forth new life and beauty.

106. I feel fortunate to live a life filled with meaning and purpose.

107. I am thankful for the chance to become part of something bigger than myself.

108. I appreciate finding pleasant moments when they are least expected.

109. I am already grateful for the amazing moments that are coming in my future.

110. I am thankful to be able to use every experience in my life to make me a better person.

111. I am thankful to be able to use every experience in my life to teach others to be better people.

112. I am grateful for the nutrition and deliciousness that food provides to make me look and feel good.

113. I appreciate the freedom I have to choose my own path in life.

114. I appreciate every compliment I receive from others to brighten my day.

115. I am thankful for the ability to envision success and the conviction to follow through and make it happen.

116. I feel grateful that there are always opportunities available to me to better myself.

117. I appreciate having access to conveniences I often take for granted like clean drinking water, indoor plumbing, and electricity.

118. I am grateful to have enough food to maintain the health and nourishment of my body.

119. I make an effort to thank every single person who has made a positive impact on my life.

120. I am thankful for all the adventures I have embarked upon.

121. I feel grateful for kind gestures from the random strangers that I meet.

122. I feel fortunate for the overflowing happiness that I have to offer others.

123. I am grateful for every day I wake up to greet the sunrise.

124. I appreciate the satisfied feeling that comes with an honest day's hard work.

125. I am thankful for all the special things, big and small, that make life worth living.

126. I am grateful that something as simple as saying "thank you" can lead to happiness.

127. I feel grateful to live in a time when I can instantly and easily communicate with my friends, family, and loved ones.

128. I appreciate my daily routines that start and end my days right.

129. I am grateful for the quality content that other people have shared on the internet that opens my mind to new things.

130. I am grateful for a time of rest after a time of work.

131. I am thankful to have people in my life who love me unconditionally.

132. I appreciate my freedom to be myself and express my individuality.

133. I am grateful for the technological innovations that make my life more convenient.

134. I feel fortunate for all the role models who have served as a positive influence in my life.

135. For the insight I acquire from people who have gone through what I am currently going through, I am really grateful to them.

136. I am grateful for my ability to find the silver lining in everything.

137.   I am thankful for life's teachable moments that provide me with valuable lessons.

138.   I appreciate overcast days because they make me even more grateful for sunny weather.

Chapter 28
Financial Affirmations for Every Day

Financial affirmations are brief phrases you may repeat to yourself to feel better about money. Money mantras and abundance affirmations are two more names for financial affirmations that you may come across. The idea is to keep yourself motivated as you go through your financial path. A money mantra may help you remain on track to achieve your financial objectives, no matter where you are at in the process of achieving them.

It is important to remember that financial affirmations should always be delivered in a positive manner. You should refrain from being continuously judgmental of your decisions or your financial situation. Instead, adopting a positive attitude will assist you in being pleased with your financial decisions. A negative mantra might lead to bad financial choices in the future.

Maintaining a positive frame of mind should make a significant difference while trying to stay on track with your money. Although it is easy to get consumed by bad feelings when it comes to money, this negativity will not serve you well in the long run. In fact, having a negative frame of mind might keep you trapped in the same financial behaviors that aren't serving you well.

When you have a positive frame of mind, you may locate excellent things because you are actively seeking them. Instead of focusing only on your lack of progress or faults, you'll discover that it's far simpler to remark on the steps you've taken to get there.

The Affirmations

1. I am financially secure.

2. The joy I feel knows no bounds.
3. I'm capable of dealing with whatever that comes my way.
4. I always have a nice chunk of money in the bank.
5. My relationship with money is healthy and loving.
6. I am not afraid to ask for a raise when I deserve one.
7. Every day, in every aspect, I'm improving and becoming better and better.
8. I am prepared to go to any length to achieve self-sufficiency in my life.
9. I am a genius who can handle anything that comes my way.
10. I am easily able to save a portion of my income each month.
11. I have more talent inside of me than I know what to do with.
12. I deserve a good night's sleep after a long day of hard work.
13. I feel deserving of all the abundance that life has to offer.
14. I make a lot of money but never find myself lacking anything.
15. I set financial goals and work hard each day to achieve them.
16. It is easy for me to prioritize my needs and put myself first.
17. People compliment me on my hair, clothes, and spending habits.
18. All of my hard work finally paying off is an incredible feeling.

19. My best is always good enough; others recognize my worthiness.

20. being so concerned about my financial future has really paid off.

21. Every thought I think creates a new reality for me to experience.

22. In order to see my aspirations realized, I am prepared to go to any length to achieve them.

23. I measure my success by the love and happiness I have in my life.

24. I feel confident that my financial future is secure and promising.

25. I am financially independent and feel free in all aspects of money.

26. My family and friends; they are very proud of how well I handle money matters.

27. My tax obligations are up to date and I always pay my bills on time.

28. I am a genius, and everything I need to prosper is already within me.

29. I value whether or not I can afford something, not how much it costs.

30. I am able to see opportunities when they arise and capitalize on them.

31. I have the ability to negotiate my salary and never sell myself short.

32. I have achieved great success and satisfaction in every aspect of my life to date.

33. The more successful I become, the less time I have for boredom or worry.

34. I have the power and will never give up or let anyone tell me otherwise.

35. I'm grateful for this moment, but it doesn't define where I'll be tomorrow.

36. As I learn more about managing money, my money skills increase even further.

37. I can be as great as I want to be, if only I believe in my power to achieve.

38. I deserve to be successful in all aspects of my life, especially with money.

39. My income is higher than my expenses and I am not struggling to stay afloat.

40. I use money to express myself in whatever way I want and make the most of it.

41. I am aware of the impact that making good financial choices can have on my life.

42. I am becoming more financially stable every day, as long as I keep working hard.

43. My worth does not come from how much money I make but from who I am as a person.

44. I am able to actually provide for my family and make them proud with what I have achieved.

45. Every day, I am grateful for all of the opportunities that hard work has given me.

46. I am able to stay grounded when thinking about money and make decisions with ease.

47. Today I will do what others won't, so tomorrow I can accomplish what others can't.

48. It feels good to have my own savings put away and I enjoy how it builds up each day.

49. Money now flows to me freely and without effort. I am open to receiving it in whatever shape that it may take.

50. I am open-minded when thinking about money and willing to learn more about the topic.

51. Spending money on others brings me a lot of joy, but it's important to save some too.

52. I feel a sense of pride in all that I have accomplished and the time it took to do so.

53. Money doesn't make me happy or sad, but I feel really good when spending it on others.

54. There is really no obstacle that big enough to stop me from succeeding at whatever I choose to do.

55. I am determined to build wealth so one day I can help those less fortunate than myself.

56. I have a healthy relationship with money and make smart choices in how I spend my money.

57. My savings account is as full as it was the day it started and every penny of it is mine.

58. Each month, I have a budget that allows me to put at least 5% of my income toward savings.

59. I deserve financial abundance and I trust in the universe to give me opportunities for it.

60. Sometimes, I make peace with my past financial mistakes and work hard to never repeat them.

61. I always learn from my mistakes because each one teaches me how not to act next time around.

62. It feels great to invest in myself by taking a course or class on a topic that interests me.

63. Other people are able to look up to me as a great role model when it comes to money matters.

64. The best investment can make is in yourself by continuously learning and honing your skills.

65. There are plenty of opportunities for everyone willing to get off their ass and go get them.

66. When it comes to properly managing my finances, I have a great deal of satisfaction in my accomplishments.

67. If I have problems, they are tiny and insignificant compared to the size of my heart and soul.

68. As a result of my fantastic credit score, I have no concern about the possibility of ever requiring good credit for anything significant.

69. Finally, the only person who stands between you and your goals is you.

70. It feels wonderful to succeed at saving money instead of spending everything I make each month.

71. Today, I make a commitment to learn about how to better handle money while having fun doing it.

72. When faced with financial decisions, I consider all available options before making a decision.

73. I am a channel of divine energy. I use my energy to manifest the life that I desire and deserve.

74. Sometimes, if an opportunity comes up that would cause me to overspend, I choose not to take it.

75. As I learn more about managing my money, I look for new ways to improve upon what I already know.

76. If I am not sure how to handle a financial situation, I ask for help from those that know better.

77. I am pleased with how much I have learnt about investing my money in various ventures throughout the course of my career.

78. I put myself first in line when thinking about spending money and wasting it on unimportant things.

79. It feels good to spend time away from home with people that are close to me enjoying life together.

80. I never go into debt without having a solid plan in place that allows me to pay off my debt quickly.

81. Saving money every month is a huge achievement and it makes me feel great to accomplish such a goal.

82. When handling my finances, it is important to be realistic about how much I have versus what I need.

83. I feel great about all of my savings accounts because they represent how much hard work has paid off.

84. I value how much enjoyment I get out of spending money on meaningful things while still being frugal.

85. I work hard at keeping my financial house in order so one day I might be able to purchase my own home.

86. When going over my finances, I am able to keep a clear head and understand where all of my money goes.

87. I am able to ask for help when I need it and know there are resources available to me when I need them.

88. When it comes to acquiring money, where you start is less important than where you want to end up at the conclusion of the process.

89. Every little bit counts when trying to build wealth because every penny saved eventually becomes dollars.

90. My checking account is often overflowing and there is always a healthy sum of cash in my savings account.

91. All of my ideas are valid regardless of how others may perceive them, especially when it comes to finances.

92. I'm grateful for what this moment brings but even more excited about all the ones still waiting ahead of me.

93. Living below your means doesn't just benefit you financially; it also improves your overall quality of life.

94. I am surrounded by abundance on all levels of my life - financially, spiritually, emotionally, and physically.

95. I leave money on the table when I could be making more by taking advantage of opportunities that come my way.

96. I never regret trusting my instincts when it comes to money matters and know that it is always best to do so.

97. Sometimes what you have to do isn't fun, but it has to be done because the result is worth all of the effort.

98. When it comes to saving money, I always make sure to budget everything out and not go overboard with spending.

99. Having good credit represents how responsible I have been overall with my finances which also means a lot to me.

100. Although I am not perfect with money management, I know that I am always improving myself more and more each day.

101. I am proud of my new-found financial knowledge and how much more comfortable it has made me feel about my future.

102. I love the feeling of freedom that money provides me with. The less I worry about money, the more freedom I have.

103. Investing in myself by learning new skills or getting certifications look great on paper when applying for a job.

104. I realized that being broke isn't about how much you earn or spend, but rather what mindset is attached to it all.

105. The more relaxed I am about money, the wealthier I become. I am abundant and can receive more whenever I want it.

106. Every day brings new opportunities for me. The more I relax about money, the more money comes into my experience.

107. I never ever let money stand in the way of something that is important to me and feel lucky to be able to afford it all.

108. Just because I don't have a lot of money doesn't mean that I can't enjoy my life and appreciate everything around me.

109. Just because my bank account isn't overflowing with cash doesn't mean I can't still celebrate all I have in life.

110. When faced with financial problems, I consider every option available and find the best one suited for me.

111. Combining my finances with someone else's is very stressful and makes me uncomfortable, so I keep them separate for now.

112. I am making choices today that will positively impact my financial state tomorrow. Save now so you can spend more later.

113. Being financially secure allows me the freedom to work on achieving other life goals such as buying a house or traveling.

114. Debt relief is like to climbing a mountain; it's tedious and arduous, but the view from the summit is well worth it.

115. When thinking about financial problems, I take a step back and examine all of my options before making any rash decisions.

116. Being broke sucks, but there are many like me who can relate to how difficult life is when you have no money in your pocket.

117. I am grateful for all the money I have right now. As I focus on having more, it comes into my life easily and effortlessly.

118. I really don't need a lot of money to be happy, I just prefer having more than enough because life is easier when you have options.

119. Reaching out for help is a sign of strength not weakness, and knowing I have a solid support system makes everything easier.

120. Every month, I put aside a particular amount of money for savings first, before spending the remaining on bills and other frivolous expenditures like entertainment.

121. I am grateful for money because it gives me the freedom to do whatever I want without worrying about how much anything costs.

122. I am always very proud of how well I handle money matters because being financially responsible helps me succeed in all parts of my life.

123. Every day miracles happen in my life, including financial miracles. I am grateful for all the money coming to me right now.

124. My roommate/landlord/significant other understands my situation and helps me out until things get better financially on my end.

125. It has been shown that taking care of myself physically helps me feel better emotionally, so I indulge myself by purchasing something expensive every now and again to reward myself.

126. When you're fit and healthy, you're able to be productive. This is essential for business and will help me make more money.

127. Having a lot of free time allows me to relax and unwind without feeling guilty about wasting too much time doing nothing at all.

128. When faced with financial problems, I take a step back and analyze my options instead of panicking and doing something I will regret.

129. My relationship with money is joyful and completely free of fear. Money comes easily to me now, and there's plenty for everyone.

130. When faced with financial problems, I take a step back and contemplate what the best decision would be for my overall well-being.

131. Getting over financial problems is not as stressful as before now that I know what needs to be done in order to improve upon them.

132. My job is fun because it's a way of expressing myself and sharing what I have to offer with others.

133. I am making plans for increasing my income. I create new ideas every day that will help me gain more money, without hurting anyone.

134. It's okay if things don't go according to plan sometimes because the only way to learn from our mistakes is through trial and error.

135. My past mistakes taught me a lot about making better decisions moving forward without repeating the same, self-destructive behavior.

136. Even though my bank account doesn't reflect my financial success, I know that with enough time my efforts will show tangible results.

137. Money is always a good servant but a bad master. I choose to let go of any greed, jealousy or envy so that I can experience true prosperity.

138. When giving to others, I make sure it is something they really need instead of something I want to give them because I can afford it.

139. In order to make more sustainable financial progress, I need focus on all aspects of budgeting from spending to saving to giving back.

140. My personal relationships are very important, and I would never jeopardize them for money at all because I value them much more than that.

141. The money that I have now is bringing me comfort and security, and the extra advice of my accountant is helping me to plan for my future.

142. It is amazing how much money I am able to save and spend on things by simply planning ahead. It's just so easy when you know what you're doing.

143. I am open to receiving all the money I deserve and more, as life struggles make me stronger and help me grow wiser and cleverer each day.

144. Money is a neutral force in my life that neither brings me happiness nor sadness, but sometimes it makes me happy when spending it on others.

145. Every day I get better at managing what belongs to me… including money. As I grow wealthy, everyone benefits from being associated with me.

146. Happiness always comes from within and not from materialistic items that cost a bunch of money that will only bring me temporary satisfaction anyway.

147. I am consistently working towards my financial goals and targets because I enjoy the feeling of success that comes when I receive a paycheck.

148. Being financially free means that you don't ever have to answer to anyone or do something that you don't want to do in order to earn your keep.

149. I am realizing that my own deeds are the only ones that can affect how much money will come to me – no one gets rich by sitting on their hands.

150. People die with their wealth too often than not, so if I continue to save then someday, I'll be able to leave something behind for other people.

151. People love me unconditionally just as I love myself unconditionally. We all have our own different flaws, but we also have so many wonderful qualities too.

152. Even though I can't afford it right now, I don't let that stop me from wanting to buy the things that brighten up my day and add value to my life.

153. Figuring out how much I can save each month has been tough, but if it's challenging then it must mean that the rewards are proportionally greater?

154. I allow abundance into my life easily and effortlessly now. It is my divine right to have an overflow of wealth, happiness, health, and prosperity.

155. I am doing my best every day with money because it's the only way to ensure a comfortable life. Money isn't everything; but you can't buy happiness.

156. I am growing in knowledge about money every day, and this helps me plan for the future. My savings will work hard to provide for me later on in life.

157. It's easy to save money when you remember that everything is temporary. It all comes and goes, so why should the things that matter be any different?

158. I am talented in many areas that I fail to recognize. I take this opportunity now to uncover my talents and use them for the greater good of humanity.

159. I don't need a lot of money or expensive possessions to prove that I'm rich because being rich means having about the freedom to do whatever makes me happy.

160. My whole life I've been learning about money, and it's finally paying off in a big way. At this rate, my children will probably be wealthier than I am.

161. When I learn how to make money work for me, it's amazing. It's taken a lot of effort on my part, but I can see the payoff more and more as time goes on.

162. My new thoughts and feelings create the reality of my dreams. Every day miracles happen in my life, as long as I focus on all that is good and positive.

163. I am always doing my best every day with money because I know that it dictates how I'll live in the future. Money isn't one's everything, but it sure is a lot of fun.

164. I deserve to be happy with money in my life like everyone else. Sure, it isn't the most essential thing in the world, but why should it be handled any differently from the rest of life?

165. The one and the only thing stopping me from being rich is my ability to earn money, so I'm going to continue doing just that until one day I finally succeed big time.

166. I deserve the best now. I accept only good things into my life now. Abundance flows naturally to me. I am wealthy because I affirm myself as being wealthy.

167. I deserve to be happy with my money, and I'm going to go out of my way to treat myself more often. Life is just too brief not to take pleasure in things such as large purchases.

168. The most important decision you will ever make is who you allow in your life, no matter how much money you or they have or what their material possessions might be.

169. When you invest your savings properly, you should see it work hard for you. This means that you can take a step back and let it do its thing while you relax.

170. It feels amazing once you finally start earning an income because now you can do things without feeling guilty or scared about spending your hard-earned money.

171. When I spend time thinking about my savings, it makes me so happy. It really is a lot of money, and I feel so fortunate to have been able to save all of it up.

172. I am really enjoying the fruits of my labor as I start dreaming about what's next. My hard work is working hard for me now, and even better things will be coming soon.

173. I am working hard with money so that I can enjoy life's luxuries later on in life. If you cut back now, you'll have plenty of room to splurge when you're older.

174. Before I go to sleep every day, I read an article about how to attract money while sleeping. The more I learn about the laws of the universe, the better my life will run.

175. My money-making opportunities are increasing by the day, as well as my income. The right time to make a lucrative deal is approaching, and I am ready to seize it.

176. The more responsibility I gain at work, the more money I can make. My boss is counting on me, which means he will give me all the opportunities I need to succeed.

177. I am learning how to save money every day so that I can enjoy all the things I really want later on. You can't go anywhere if you don't have any money, so save up.

178.　　I happily complete all tasks that come up on my path. All those who surround me are happy because we have a healthy relationship with each other and our finances.

179.　　Some of the most important lessons you'll encounter in life are learned through mistakes, but it's our actions or reactions after making those mistakes that define who we truly are.

180.　　When it comes down to it, the harder I work for money, the more money I'll be able to make because effort eventually turns into results when enough time has passed.

181.　　I am taking care of my money now so that it can help me later on. It's easy to save if you just say no when tempted to buy something that isn't absolutely necessary.

182.　　I am learning about the importance of money in my life, and I am getting better at managing it every day. Money isn't going be your everything, but it is necessary to know when to utilize it effectively.

183.　　It feels amazing when I buy things for myself because it means I'm taking care of myself. When it comes to life, what's the purpose if you don't indulge yourself every now and then?

184.　　When I build my savings account slowly over time, there's something quite satisfying about watching it grow. It's very nice to have a nest egg in case anything awful happens.

185.　　Building wealth isn't easy, but neither is any worthwhile endeavor, and if success were as simple as working hard then everyone would actually attain their dreams easily.

186. My finances are steadily increasing as my business expands and becomes more profitable. The more people I reach with my products and services, the more I am able to earn.

187. The first step towards financial success is to simply stop spending money on things that don't matter and wasting money on living a lifestyle that doesn't suit your needs.

188. I am doing my very best every day with money because looking after your future is so very important. If you cut back now, you'll have plenty of room to splurge when you're older.

189. I am grateful for all the money coming to me right now, bringing me freedom from the bondage of old beliefs. Money flows into my life with ease, abundance and prosperity.

190. I am doing my best to be responsible with money so that I can enjoy all of life's luxuries later on in life. Sometimes you have to work for a little while before you can play.

191. I am always doing my very best every day with money because financial security is so very important. You will actually never know what life will throw at you, so having savings on hand just makes sense.

192. I deserve to be happy with money in my life, and I'm going to make sure that happens by following a budget and cutting all of the unnecessary costs. It's easier than it sounds.

193. I deserve to feel good about myself, and I'm going to make a point of getting what I want out of life. Money comes first: you can't enjoy yourself if you don't have any money.

194. Living below our means affords us room in our budget to save for future purchases or invest in ourselves. We are

selective with what we buy because we value our time and money.

195. Money is nothing but a tool that allows us to make our dreams come true. Each and every dollar has spiritual value. I am rich, and money comes to me easily and effortlessly now.

196. At this point in my life my bank account is empty, but I still have all of my internal resources available so it's just a matter of time before financial success is finally mine.

197. When I learn more about investing, I am filled with a sense of power. By learning what works and what doesn't, I am giving myself the chance to really improve my money situation.

198. When we start earning more, we think we can spend our way into happiness, but eventually we learn that the more money you make the more you end up spending it instead of saving it.

199. I deserve to be happy about my savings, and I'm going to make sure that happens by using coupons and only buying the things that I need. It's a great feeling when you get it right.

200. I'm learning so much about money every day, but I still have so much more to learn. There's always something new about numbers, even if you've been studying them for over 10 years.

201. Once my job is decentralized, I will be able to work anywhere in the world. I am becoming more financially stable by expanding my abilities and opening myself up to new experiences.

202. When I finally understand the financial markets and how they work, it's a huge relief. Knowing that there's someone

else who can help me with money and investments would be amazing.

203. I am doing everything I can to make sure I'm financially responsible because it's the only way to ensure a comfortable life. Money isn't everything since you can't buy happiness.

204. I deserve to be happy with my financial situation because everyone else is. There's no point falling behind on your savings and investments because it takes a long time to catch up.

205. I know how to create a budget that works because I take control of my finances now. My income exceeds my expenditures; I allow myself to indulge in small ways because of what I save.

206. I am always doing my very best every day with money because looking after your future is so very important. You will never ever know what life will throw at you, so having savings on hand just makes sense.

207. Getting out of debt is like climbing out from underneath a huge pile of dirt; at first it seems impossible but as soon as you make some progress, everything becomes easier and clearer.

208. My income is increasing by taking on more responsibility. I am finding that this makes my work days much more enjoyable. There is nothing better than knowing you're good at your job.

209. When I make tough decisions about my finances and they work out for the best, it feels amazing. I know that it's the result of long-term planning, and that really is making a difference.

210. I am working towards my dreams every day, and the financial gain is an ongoing perk of doing what I love. The sooner you start following your passion, the better off you'll be financially.

211. I deserve to be happy about my spending habits, and I'm going to make sure that happens by using coupons and only buying the things that I need. It's a great feeling when you get it right.

212. I am doing my best every day with money because looking after your future is more important than anything else. If you cut back now, you'll have plenty of room to splurge when you're older.

213. We value our financial assets wisely. I responsibly save my money now. Spending less than you earn is the road to wealth; saving more than you spend will always be rewarded in the future.

214. I deserve to be happy with what I have because everyone deserves a little luxury now and then. It feels so great to treat yourself to something nice every now and again, I'm so glad that I can.

215. Every day, I put out my best effort in terms of finances since financial stability is something that everyone deserves. Because you will never know what life may throw at you, it is always a good idea to have some money saved up.

216. I am taking care of my mental health every day by eating right and exercising regularly. When everything inside of me is in working order, not only is my body healthier, but my mind is also lot more at peace.

217. Money flows through me with ease and grace. Everything works out well for me. Each time I spend money, even on simple pleasures, I get something back in return... usually something better.

218. The literal definition of being successful is simply to have succeeded, so even though I haven't achieved everything I want to right now, I still believe that one day my efforts will pay off.

219. I trust that as the energy of money flows into my life, it will provide all I need. As I take responsibility for managing what already belongs to me, even better things come to me now.

220. My hobbies and passions are expensive, but that doesn't mean that I shouldn't keep doing them even if they aren't always affordable. The cost of fun isn't equivalent to the value of happiness.

221. The more money I have, the less important my physical needs become. As I become more prosperous, others benefit from being associated with me because they know that they will also be rich.

222. I deserve the best in life just like everyone else, and that includes having a proper savings account for emergencies. When life is difficult, you want to depend on friends and family.

223. I know how to set boundaries with people, places, and things. No one can make me feel loved or worthy unless I allow it. With great power comes great responsibility- so I responsibly choose love.

224. When I think about how much money I have waiting for me from my retirement fund, it makes me so happy. It really is a lot of money, and I feel so fortunate to have been able to save all of it up.

225. I'm taking full advantage of all life has to offer, without a care in the world about the future or any regrets about the past. Money is coming into my life in many different ways, and I will enjoy spending it when the time comes.

226. I am proud of my efforts towards self-improvement every day, but I will continue to work hard until I am the best version of myself. This old cliché is true: you can never be too rich or too thin.

227. When I think about how much money I have waiting for me from my retirement fund, it's so overwhelming. It really is a lot of money, and I feel so privileged to have been able to save all of it up.

228. Charity really does feel good. Knowing that by spending time or money on someone else, I'm making a difference, lifts my spirits. In our world, so many people need help, and it is a very rewarding experience to be able to help them.

229. There are no problems with my finances now...only solutions. The more responsible we are with our spending habits, the easier it is to save. I know that money comes easily and effortlessly to me now.

230. I am doing my best every day with money because looking after your future is more important than anything else. It's nice to know that if something awful happens, I can at least rely on my savings for support.

231. Every day, I put out my best effort in terms of finances since planning for your future is quite vital. You don't want to pass on debts and problems onto your children and grandchildren because you were irresponsible.

232. The more time I devote to my goals, the more likely it is that they will appear in my life. The universe is now giving me everything I want and desire. Life loves me, and money comes easily to those who love life.

233. My goal is always to make more money instead of spending money on items that are not important or necessary for happiness. My family wants for nothing because we know how to be happy without retail therapy.

234. I deserve to be happy with my financial situation because everyone else is. There's no point in being stuck in debt when there are so many other options available to you, especially if you work hard to improve it.

235. As I express gratitude for what money has already brought me, it exponentially increases in my life. Money flows from many sources. Every day more and more opportunities come my way, which brings me wealth.

236. Life has been hard for me in the past, but now it has been easy since I have learned from those circumstances. In the end, there is really no need for me to be anxious about things that are beyond of my control since everything will work out in my favor in due course.

237. We are smart about our finances; we use cash instead of credit cards. Wealth flows naturally to me now. Money comes easily and effortlessly to us now; we see money everywhere. Retirement accounts grow bigger and bigger.

238. I am grateful for this healthy relationship with money, which further strengthens our connection. Whatever my mind conceives and believes, my body experiences. Whatever I feel in my body affects every aspect of my being.

239. We are smart about our finances; we use cash instead of credit cards. Wealth flows naturally to me now. Money comes easily and effortlessly to us now; it's never scarce or lacking. We all deserve to be happy with what we have.

240. I am smart about how I invest my money so that it can last forever. I take responsibility for how much money is in my bank account. We all deserve to be financially secure and comfortable with no debt and a healthy savings account.

241. I do not want to become a billionaire solely for the purpose of being a millionaire; rather, I want to be able to live comfortably with enough savings and assets built so that I will never ever have to worry about anything else in my life.

242. We are intelligent about our investments. The more we invest, the more money we see in our bank accounts. I avoid buying luxury items because they aren't important to me. I choose to spend my money on experiences with loved ones instead.

243. I give myself permission to be open. I give myself permission to express my love, and joy. As I am open to new possibilities, the world opens up for me. The more I am open with my true self, the easier it is to connect with others.

244. The universe provides for me; money flows easily into my life now. Money comes to me freely and effortlessly right when I need it. If there is a delay in manifesting money, it is because the universe knows I have better things to do with my time.

245. Everyone on this planet is connected by an infinite source of supply. This supply never runs out; it can only multiply like a snowball rolling down a mountain. As I focus on

the abundance of this universe, it naturally transfers into my own life.

246. I am rich, and money comes to me easily and effortlessly now. Money is not here for us to judge; it's a tool that allows us to make our dreams come true. I always have enough money to cover all of life's expenses- so I don't worry about the future.

247. I trust that as the energy of money flows into my life, it will provide all that I need. As I take responsibility for managing what already belongs to me, even better things come to me now. My income keeps increasing, bringing more and more abundance with it.

248. In the evening, I always read an article on how to attract money while sleeping before going to bed. The more I learn about the laws of the universe, the better my life will run. My relationship with money is joyful and completely free of fear. Money comes easily to me now, and there's plenty for everyone.

249. My spending habits are healthy because they bring joy and nourishment to my body and mind. Money isn't earned to be saved: its purpose is to flow freely between human beings so we just can all benefit from each other's talents.

250. I will receive everything back from life tenfold. Money comes easily to me now, without my having to work for it all day long. In fact, one could say that money works for me. The more values I share with the world, the more valuable I feel. Everything I give away makes room for something better in my life.

251. Everything I give away makes room for something greater to flow in.

252.   People feel comfortable around me because they know I will never judge them or ask anything from them. Money flows toward those who do not cling to it like a child with a new toy, but those who project an attitude of gratitude toward the material things. The more we give away, the richer our lives become.

253.   It feels natural for me to help people in need because they are part of me. There is no "other" here, just existence coming through all beings continuously. you give what you want to receive, and I want to give love. As I express my gratitude, all that is mine by divine right flows back to me in generous measure.

254.   Anything I put my attention on seems to expand in front of me. The more money I make, the easier it is for me to make even more money. This cycle actually just repeats itself over and over again. My job is fun because it's a way of expressing myself and sharing what I have to offer with others. Today, as gladly as possible,

255.   I am smart about my finances; I use cash instead of credit card debts. Wealth flows naturally to me now. The universe rewards us for being responsible with our spending habits by always having enough to cover all of life's expenses - so I don't worry about the future. I am safe, secure, and taken care of 100% of the time.

256.   My creativity comes up with new ideas for earning money. The more I earn, the more I can give away. All good things come to me easily now. Everything in the universe is energy, including money. If I believe it and feel it, it will be so. The very fact that I have a good attitude about money has made my life full of happiness and fun.

257. I am at peace with money and what it represents: freedom and power. Money allows me to travel the world, spend time with friends and family, enjoy nature, pursue hobbies, and pay bills without worrying about not having enough. We all desire for a good life just as long as we use cash instead of credit cards so we can stay out of debt.

258. I deserve to be well paid for my work, and I am open to receiving more tasks that fulfill me and make the world a better place. As I focus on my abundance, I allow myself to accept more opportunities like this. They come to all those who believe in their own worth and take care of their finances. The universe is abundant; there is always enough for everyone.

259. I am a magnet for financial abundance. The more I give, the greater I get. Money is now flowing to me freely and readily. I have enough money to save for retirement or buy whatever I desire without worrying about not being able to pay my bills. My talent is living well below our means. We all deserve a luxurious life just as long as we don't go into debt doing so.

260. My income keeps increasing, bringing more and more abundance. My spending habits are healthy because they bring joy and nourishment to my body and mind.

261. The more responsible we are with our spending, the easier it is to save money. We breathe easy knowing that our families will always come first, so we save enough money for them without worry. There are delays in the manifestation of my finances only when they are perfectly aligned for my highest good and not because there is lack or scarcity. Each and every dollar has spiritual value.

262. We all breathe easy knowing our financial futures are never uncertain. We breathe easy knowing that our families will always come first, so we save enough money for them without

worry. The more responsible we are with our spending habits, the easier it is to save money. The universe rewards us for being responsible with our spending habits by always having enough money to cover all of life's expenses.

263. The more our gratitude for what we have, the more prosperous our lives become. There is abundance in everything - not just material things. We know that experiences with family and friends are what truly matter; therefor, our incomes allow us to travel whenever possible. We all deserve a luxurious life as long as we don't go into debt doing so. The universe has my back when it comes to my finances. I trust myself totally.

264. I am always financially secure, no matter what. I really deserve to live a life of abundance, and money comes to me easily and effortlessly now. Money is energy; it has no power over me because everything I need always comes to me, right at the perfect time. There are delays in the manifestation of my finances only when they are perfectly aligned for my highest good and not because there is lack or scarcity. I love how abundant my life truly is.

265. We find joy in saving money we earned because we know financial freedom will always come to us if we keep diligent with our spending habits. My family has learned the power of non-materialistic happiness, which allows us to give generously to others without worry. Money now pours into my life freely and readily; it is never sparse or missing in my life anymore. If there are delays, it is because the universe knows that life is short - so spend your time wisely doing what makes you happy.

266. Our lives are abundant in happiness, love, and gratitude; the more thankful we are for what we have, the wealthier life becomes. Money is nothing but a tool that allows us to make dreams come true. Recognizing that every dollar has spiritual significance, we accept responsibility for our own financial

well-being. Every dollar is an opportunity to practice mindfulness in action. If there are delays, it's because the universe knows that patience is always rewarded when you invest in your future self. We all deserve to be happy with what we have.

267. There are delays in the manifestation of my finances only when they are perfectly aligned for my highest good- not because there is lack or scarcity. Money is nothing but a tool that allows us to make dreams come true. Recognizing that every dollar has spiritual significance, we accept responsibility for our own financial well-being. Every dollar is an opportunity to practice mindfulness in action. If there are delays, it's because the universe knows that patience is always rewarded when you invest in your future self. There is abundance in everything, not just material things. We deserve to live a life of luxury and opulence as long as we don't go into debt doing so. Money comes easily and effortlessly to us now; it's never scarce or lacking.

Chapter 29
Breaking Bad Habits

Habits are instilled behaviors. They have been repeated so many times, day after day, that they resemble mechanical functions. You don't have to think about your habits before engaging in them. You will learn the importance of knowing which of your behaviors must be eliminated. You can learn to mine the good aspects of complex behavior since it can have both good and bad effects.

In his book, Affirmations, Wilde suggests that the world around us actively works to undermine or destroy our power or sense of personal control. Then, affirmations of strength and control allow their bearer to overcome society's most imposing obstacles (Wilde, 2009). The affirmations will focus on the often lengthy and arduous process of reprogramming one's behavior. While difficult, this process is imminently worthwhile.

The Affirmations

1. *Your behavior is completely within your control.*

It is important to realize that how we behave is entirely within our control despite what we may think. Except for yourself, there is no one else to blame for the things you do and say in your life. You need to take responsibility.

2. *Everything you do should improve your life and the lives of others.*

Your actions should be purposeful. Why act without purpose? You are how you behave; and every action you take should in some way reflect your deepest values and desires. Give thought to your actions. Why are you behaving this way? Should you modify your behavior?

3. *You will stop behaving in destructive ways.*

Identify the moments in your life in which you act in harmful ways to yourself or the people around you. Do you know that you are in complete control of the actions you take, so why behave in destructive ways? You have no excuse for behaving poorly. It's on you.

4. *If you repeat a bad behavior, simply notice and ask yourself to do differently next time. You understand and forgive yourself.*

You must not treat yourself harshly. You will learn best from reinforcing good behaviors, not from punishing yourself for bad ones.

5. *With time and perseverance, you will transform yourself.*

Confidence in your ability to attain your objectives is essential. Believing that you are capable is powerful and will help you to manifest your desired result more easily and in less time. You are capable of it.

6. *Make a list of your bad habits. You understand that to combat bad behaviors, you must first acknowledge them.*

What habits do you wish to rid yourself of? What are the effects of these habits? In recognizing the specific nature of our most destructive habits, we can better confront them. You don't have to be scared of your behaviors. Put them to paper, and in so doing realize how small they are.

7. *You will slowly abandon all of the most harmful parts of yourself. You will feel freer.*

There is nothing quite so freeing as proving to yourself that the behavioral loops you feel "stuck" within don't have so great a hold on you. You are capable of change. People do change. All it takes is a certain strength and willingness.

8. *You are capable of overcoming established habits. It only takes time.*

the secret is time. You must strive to never lose patience with or hope for yourself. You must never give up. The only obstacle to your enduring and meaningful change is you.

9. *Today, you are grateful to yourself for trying to change for the better.*

It is important to recognize the effort you expend and the strides (however great or small) you make. Too often, we forget to reward ourselves or to appreciate ourselves for our work. Make sure you don't.

10. *You will learn more about yourself and your habits every day.*

You are observant and intelligent. That's not an opinion: it's a fact. You are capable of learning and growing; you are capable. Make a conscious effort to notice the way you act and think. Every bit of information can help you.

11. *You can unlearn your most destructive behaviors. You will.*

Believe in yourself. It will take time, but you have that time to give. Destructive behaviors can be rooted deep within ourselves. It takes hard work and sometimes a struggle to unlearn awful habits. You have to know that you are capable of it.

12. *Your willingness to evaluate yourself is admirable.*

A lot of people have trouble with honestly confronting their worst habits. We are hyper-critical, but at the same time, unwilling to tackle the parts of ourselves that are truly detrimental. Make sure you are not like that and you confront and eliminate your worst qualities.

> 13. *You have made a difference in yourself and the way you move through this world. You will continue to do so.*

Notice and appreciate, from time to time, the strides you have made. You are a different person than you were a couple of weeks ago. How do you feel about these small changes? What changes do you want to see a couple of weeks from now?

> 14. *You are embracing every small chance to improve yourself.*

Sometimes, we let the chance to change pass us by. Not today. Whenever there's an opportunity to behave in a way that aligns with your goals, seize it. You make sure that every one of your actions counts.

> 15. *You are dynamic.*

You are not doomed to remain the same forever. In fact, remaining the same is a near-impossible thing to do. Take control of the change in yourself and push yourself to change in the manner you want.

> 16. *You will determine which of your negative habits and deconstruct those.*

You can identify the habits that are harmful to you or rooted in a harmful attitude. You can then discourage yourself from behaving in that way again.

> 17. *Your behavior changes as your thoughts change. You will think more positive and helpful ways. You will give yourself credit for having beneficial thought processes.*

It's not always possible to be self-aware all the time, to know for certain why we are doing certain things. However, it is possible to encourage yourself to think more positively. This positive thinking will affect your actions in a similarly positive way.

> 18. *You will let go of the thoughts that are holding you back from your full potential.*

Once you have identified a thought process that only serves to harm you, banish it from your mind and heart. You do not want to create more obstacles for yourself. Make room for new, more helpful thoughts.

> 19. *You are making room for new, constructive habits.*

Breaking old habits means making new ones that promote your success. See the good that comes, or could potentially come, from cutting out bad habits and bad frames of mind.

> 20. *Your day is filled with wonderful change.*

Change is such a beautiful thing. You know that your life is surrounded by, and infused by, a wonderful dynamicity. Observe the change you see in your environment or in the people all around you. Be this change.

> 21. *Habits are entrenched behaviors. You recognize that unraveling these will take a great deal of time.*

Patience, patience, patience. You've got all the patience in the world, my friend. Trust in yourself and your ability to get to where you are going. Nothing you desire should come to you immediately. Where is the lesson in immediate gratification?

> 22. *You are not controlled or defined by your most negative habits.*

Your negative habits are a part of you, but they do not define you. You are so much more than a few paltry bad habits.

> 23. *You are proud of yourself for your valiant and consistent efforts.*

It takes a lot out of a person, being strong and courageous every day. Yet somehow, you can manage it. Take today to be proud of your strength of body and mind. You deserve to take pride in who you are.

> *24. You are stronger than your worst habits and your most consuming addictions. You will overcome them.*

No matter the behavior, you can stop it. No matter what. Any belief toward the contrary is a straight-up fallacy. Close your eyes and say it once more: You are stronger. You will overcome.

> *25. You choose to improve yourself and feel better for having done so.*

There's a lot of power in choice. These changes in you are all a product of your choices. You choose the change. Remember that and make good choices every single day.

> *26. You consciously recognize the most pervasive of your bad behaviors. Slowly, you make sure even these are completely eliminated.*

To get rid of your bad behaviors, you must be conscious of them. You have to point them out to yourself whenever they recur and ask yourself to do better next time. This is the only way.

> *27. You overcome adversity. You welcome the challenge.*

It's all about your state of mind. Any difficult task is far less imposing if you become excited by the prospect of victory. Let yourself get competitive. Let yourself be electrified at the idea of winning.

> *28. You are grateful for your ability to change and grow.*

Imagine always being the same. You are grateful that the world doesn't work that way and that you have the power to be whatever you want to be.

29. You will release the habits that no longer or never have propped you up.

You do not need useless and ugly things. You let go. You're better for having let go.

Chapter 30
Building Constructive Habits

Now that you have deconstructed destructive behaviors, it's time to move on to replace them with new, more productive behaviors. At the start, sticking to your habits can be extremely challenging. When you are building a new habit, the most labor-intensive period is the phase of establishment. You must expend conscious thought and effort to repeat the desirable behavior. After this period has ended, however, you will be able to repeat the behavior without consciously thinking about it. When a desirable behavior becomes a habit, it is no longer difficult to keep it up.

In their study, "Pro-Environmental Actions, Climate Change, and Defensiveness: Do Self-Affirmations Make a Difference to People's Motives and Beliefs About Making a Difference?" authors Sparks, Jessop, Chapman, and Holmes found that self-affirmations had a real, demonstrable effect on the participants. Those who used self-affirmations to motivate their behavior and manipulate their intentions showed increased engagement with desirable behaviors.

Specifically, the authors observe that positive self-affirmations can push people to recycle more frequently. There is a scientific basis for the effectiveness of positive self-affirmation. When we tap into the potential of positive self-talk, we can improve our behaviors and build long-lasting habits that promote our health and productivity.

The Affirmations

1. *You are determined to build good habits that help you to live a better, more fulfilling life.*

Never underestimate the importance of determination. This is the quality that will carry you to the finish line. You refuse to quit! You refuse to let those obstacles overwhelm you as you strive to meet your goals! Nothing can stop you if you don't allow it to!

2. *You will do right by yourself today.*

To "do right by yourself" means acting in ways that honor your desires and your basic needs. You should strive to do right by yourself every day, and thus act in ways that align with your goals.

3. *You will give your body adequate food and rest.*

In pursuit of broader, less tangible goals, we might forget to honor our bodies. Your mind requires adequate nutrition and rest to function properly. Make sure that you are eating and sleeping enough. Make certain that what you consume will leave you feeling well in the long run.

4. *You are creative and inventive. You will determine what habits are most enriching for you.*

You cannot expect to implement the best possible habits overnight. It takes thought to figure out what habits you would most like to learn. It also takes trial and error. You will discover, over time, what works well for you in your life.

5. *Your habits will reflect on you positively.*

When you have developed the right and most positive habits, people will notice and admire you for it. Your mannerisms will set you apart from the rest of the group. They will make you a desirable partner, friend, and family member.

6. *You will only engage in behaviors that help you lead a better life.*

Today, focus your energy on your goals so that you can behave in the best possible ways. The more you practice this focus, the stronger it will become and the better your behavior will be. Have faith in your process.

7. *You will respect the work you put in to develop good habits.*

Don't let anyone, least of all yourself, make you doubt yourself. You are trying to become better. So, every day, become a little better than the day before. Internalize this fact. Allow no one to deceive you into believing anything that is not true.

8. *You establish healthy and productive habits on a daily basis. You are filled with determination.*

Consistency is key. There is consistency in many things it is all around you. For example, you can be sure the sun will rise tomorrow. You can be sure the seasons will change. If your heart continues to beat, you may be certain that you are still alive. So, be sure that your effort to change remains consistent.

9. *You are taking control of the way you behave.*

It is satisfying to take control. Once you've done it, you'll wonder why you hadn't started the process years ago. If you want to get things started, there is no better moment than right now. Take a deep breath, and concentrate on trying to change one, simple thing you've decided needs to change. You can do it.

10. *You feel good for working to change yourself in small ways.*

You have earned the right to feel good. You deserve to think about your efforts and to be glad. With all that you have done, the least you deserve is that. So, smile and pat yourself on the back. Things are looking up.

11. *You find better ways to communicate your ideas with others.*

Sometimes, we struggle to articulate our thoughts inarticulate, sincere, and respectful ways. Work to communicate your ideas in the best way possible, today. People will be more receptive to your ideas and suggestions if you learn to speak well.

> 12. *You practice healthy behaviors that improve your body and mood.*

Focus on your bodily health and the quality of your mood. How might you improve these? How motivated are you to improve these? Recognize that both of these things are incredibly important to your continued success and productivity.

> 13. *You empower yourself by taking charge of your life. You are incredible.*

Feeling in control is powerful stuff. When you know you are in control and feel that power, it becomes much easier to act that way. You are no longer enslaved by the idea that you are powerless. You are no longer in your way.

> 14. *Your peers will recognize the changes you continue to make in yourself. You will feel pride in your accomplishments.*

Let others inspire you to work harder and be better. Your peers notice your continued improvement. Once in a while, they will pay you compliments for it, and you will feel great pride in the changes you have made in your life.

> 15. *You will remember to be patient with yourself. You know it takes time to develop the most useful habits to you.*

Don't rush yourself. The best things and things of the best quality take time to polish and perfect. Your progress is not too slow. If anything, know when it would be valuable to slow yourself down a bit more.

16. *You challenge yourself to remain constant in your focus, dedication, and patience.*

Consistency is important. You have to remember to reinforce good behaviors every day. The repetition of a desirable action will cement it as a habit, and habits drive you toward your goals. Remember that you are a dedicated person. You don't give up on your aspirations.

17. *Your efforts are inspiring. Give yourself the credit that you deserve.*

It takes courage and hope to work toward positive change. Be happy that you are courageous and hopeful. Drive forward in this world with the awareness that you can improve yourself with every breath you take.

18. *You know there is nothing wrong with having pride in your accomplishments.*

Be aware of your faults, be humbled by them, and proud of what you can do for yourself and others. There is nothing wrong with pride. In combination with self-awareness, Pride is a useful tool that awards us an understanding of our strenuous efforts.

19. *Today, the world is filled with opportunity. You will grasp opportunities with both hands. You will act with dignity and grace.*

Today, make sure that you focus intently. If we lose focus, great opportunities will pass us by, and we won't even notice. Make sure you do what you can for yourself.

20. *Your good habits speak to what you most value and work to make you a better person.*

You can depend on your good habits if they can depend on you. Even when you are tired, follow through on your promises to yourself. With time, it will get simpler and easier to do. Not a short time, by any means, but the ease of doing these good things is worth the work and the wait.

> 21. *You value yourself enough to make yourself better.*

It's a testament to your self-respect that you work hard to improve. Notice the kindness you show yourself and be grateful for it. You treat yourself well and you should be proud that you do. Understand that treating yourself with respect and consideration will help you improve.

> 22. *You recognize that you can improve yourself in some small way every day. You recognize that you are valuable throughout the process of self-improvement.*

Do not value the attainment of the goal more than the work you put in to get there. The work can be as pleasurable as the finished product. If you enjoy the process, the process will seem easier and will pass by more smoothly. Make every effort to discover the asset in your job.

> 23. *You love the way you are.*

You loved yourself then: you love yourself now. Do not reserve your love for who you will be. Love every version of yourself as you work to change. You aren't working to change because you hate your current self. You're working to change because you love self-improvement.

> 24. *The habits you have built make you stand out to the people around you. You are remarkable.*

People lose focus. While your peers struggle to remain mindful of their continual change, you will not. Not you. You are well aware of what is most essential. You know what you have to do to reach your goals.

> 25. *You will continually acknowledge your progress and reward yourself for it.*

Don't let your improvement go unnoticed. Your progress deserves recognition and adequate reward. This reward may come in many forms: a piece of chocolate cake, a new tattoo, a day without work. Be extra indulgent, today.

> 26. *You are determined to transform. Your concentrated willpower can achieve incredible results.*

Your determination is staggering. You know that you can do wonderful things for yourself and for others when you concentrate. Today, remind yourself that you are filled with determination. Remind yourself that your goals truly matter.

> 27. *You will let destructive urges pass over you. You will examine them with interest. You will not indulge them.*

Why do we have destructive urges? Try to unveil the root cause of your strange thoughts and desires to act poorly today. Discover why these things are a part of you. Then, ask yourself if you can do something to prevent these desires from recurring.

> 28. *You will indulge in ambitious ideas. You work toward achieving your behavioral goals.*

You may have ideas or goals that seem completely unachievable right now. That doesn't mean you will never achieve them: it means it will take your best, most amazing effort.

> 29. *You are active and intelligent.*

You are. You move, act, think. Recognize the strangeness of this miracle.

> 30. *You are passionate and genuine.*

You are. You should seek out what you are passionate about. You should say what you genuinely believe.

31. You have fantastic self-control.

Today, practice your self-control. Like anything, self-control requires a great deal of practice.

Chapter 31
On Sadness

We will all experience periods of deep sadness in our lifetimes. Some of us will experience these periods more frequently than others, but all of us will know what it means to feel deeply sad, lost, and confused. On the whole, our society does a very poor job of instructing us on how to cope with feelings of inadequacy and isolation. You will be able to experience sadness without guilt and address your sadness with the utmost effectiveness. I'm sorry to say it, but sometimes sadness needs to be felt. Through these various affirmations, you will give yourself full permission to feel sad. You will also give yourself the tools required to eventually overcome melancholy.

In their study, "Attributions and Affirmations for Overcoming Anxiety and Depression," Kinnier, Hofsess, Pongratz and Lambert (2009) discovered that positive affirmations induced in their bearers a sense of normalcy (as it relates to depression and anxiety) and were helpful to their participants' recoveries.

The Affirmations

1. *You will not blame yourself for feeling unhappy. You will not blame anyone.*

Blame is another thing that does little good, especially when it comes to addressing feelings of sadness. Do not waste your energy on finding someone to blame or making yourself feel all the worse by blaming yourself. Get rid of blame.

2. *You deserve to indulge in feelings of unhappiness from time to time.*

Sometimes being unhappy is unavoidable. Sometimes it is, but repressing that feeling will only lead to trouble down the road. Let yourself be unhappy once in a while. Letting yourself feel unhappy will help you to heal and let go of self-pity, resentment, and regret.

3. *Your unhappiness does not define you.*

You will be unhappy. That does not mean you are an unhappy person or your mood will dictate how you behave. You can overcome feelings of sadness, just as you can overcome every other feeling. It takes work and time, like everything else.

4. *You understand that feeling unhappy is normal. You understand that you are a strong person.*

You are not alone in your unhappiness. People become unhappy, sometimes. It's not actually something to be ashamed of; it's not something that will alienate you from your friends (unless you let it.) You are perfectly normal.

5. *You will appreciate negative feelings for their positive influence on you.*

Feelings of inadequacy are based on nothing at all. Still, that does not mean they are useless. Since they exist, you reframe them and use them to push yourself to improve. You may think, "I'm not fit enough." Because of that thought, you now know that you need to find a new physical activity that brings you joy. You are fit enough. However, if you want to become a better fit, there is a way to achieve it

6. *You are not alone in your unhappiness. You can comfort others; they can comfort you.*

The fact of the matter is actually that this is one of the most important things for you to remember in your most tough moments. Other people understand. Other people know what you are feeling and may talk to you about it, if only you reach out to them. For your own sake, you should do so.

7. *You understand that your sadness will end.*

Everything ends, and sadness is no different. You will not have to endure this unhappy feeling forever. Hold on for those precious moments of joy, contentedness, gratitude, and love. They are worth the wait.

8. *You accept what you cannot change. You move on.*

You have complete control over your behavior. In fact, that is all you have complete control over. There are going to be things around you that you don't like and that you can't change. Sometimes, you have to graciously accept the world for what it is. You can only do so much.

9. *Your sadness does not make you weak. You have emotional depth.*

There's nothing wrong with being sad. There's nothing abnormal about being sad. Do not compound your unhappiness by feeling ashamed of your sadness. There is absolutely nothing to be embarrassed of. Give yourself time and kindness, and you will recover.

10. *You discover the root of your unhappiness and examine it. You decide if you can make a positive change that will address these unhappy feelings.*

You can notice these feelings and ask, "Why is it I feel this way?" You can continue to ask this question until you uncover the real truth of the matter. Then, when you know the truth, you can determine if anything can be done to change the way you feel. There is no harm in trying this potentially beneficial exercise.

11. *You do not linger too long in sadness. You act to overcome these negative feelings.*

You should not dwell on the same, sad things. It's okay to be sad, but you can choose to step away from that sadness. You will really be able to dedicate more of your time and energy to other, more successful projects as a result. Sometimes, feelings of sadness will abate if you stop focusing on them.

> 12. *You understand the power of open spaces. You breathe in the fresh air with an appreciation for your ability to do so.*

Nothing is guaranteed, not even life itself. You are aware of the temporary nature of life and of everything in your life. You are ultimately grateful for what you have.

> 13. *You understand the power of the community. You lean on others when you need emotional support. This does not make you weak.*

From time to time, you are going to need a little help from your friends. Every one of us needs a little extra assistance. They can help push you to overcome feelings of melancholy.

> 14. *You endure sadness. You understand that even negative feelings can help you to improve yourself.*

It takes a lot of strength to outlast feelings of sadness. These feelings are so powerful, and devastating that they threaten to overwhelm us. However, you know you have the strength it takes to endure these feelings. No matter how long it takes, you will endure.

> 15. *You know that you will appreciate moments of joy all the more for having experienced moments of melancholy.*

To experience the highest highs of life, you have to experience the lowest lows. There is no ecstasy without suffering. There is no beauty without ugliness. There is no light without darkness. Make peace with this: You cannot appreciate the best things in life without going through the worst.

> *16. You respect yourself in your sadness. You address your sadness in the ways you find to be the kindest and appropriate.*

Do not berate yourself for feeling inadequate. This will only compound the feeling. Do not berate yourself for feeling sad. This will only compound the sadness. Know that it is all right to feel sad. Treat yourself with the utmost respect.

> *17. You know that life is the most valuable thing.*

Life is the only thing. There is nothing so precious as life. Please don't let anybody or anything to make you question this for a single second. The world is a wonderful place despite its horrors, and you want to be here.

> *18. You are grateful for the moments of melancholy. They show you how strong you are.*

It takes strength and incredible patience to get through periods of sadness. After that sadness subsides, you will know how strong you are. You will actually have a greater understanding of the power of your character.

> *19. You do not resent your sadness. You make the most of your emotions.*

You can choose to use your sadness as fuel. Sadness has been known to make people funnier, more creative, or more inventive. See what benefits you can find in your sadness. You might as well practice productivity in the most unfavorable circumstances.

> *20. You let their caring lift your spirits.*

The people in your life can lift you out from the pits of despair if you let them. You should know that these people care about you. You should understand that they want the best for you. So long as they are here, you will never be alone.

> 21. *You avoid self-pity at all costs. It is not helpful to you.*

Do not pity yourself for your sadness. You are not a pitiable thing. You are strong and in control, even in moments of weakness. Be sad if you must be, but never feel bad for yourself. This pain is only temporary. You can handle it.

> 22. *You know that healing takes time. You don't rush the process.*

Just as you practice patience for yourself in all other areas, you are patient while you are healing. It does take a good deal of time. You are ready to wait in silence. You are ready to wait a long, long time if you must.

> 23. *When faced with adversity, you know you will get through it.*

It is not blind confidence. You know yourself and your abilities intimately. Know that this period, however daunting, will not grind you down into the dust. You will bounce back stronger and more self-assured than ever before.

> 24. *You know that nothing worth having should come easily to you. You put the work in.*

You wouldn't enjoy attaining something you didn't work hard to attain. Because you know this, you don't begrudge having to work hard. You know the results will absolutely be worth this struggle and hardship!

> 25. *You forgive yourself for being sad. You recognize, now, that your sadness was reasonable all along.*

If you are suffering from depression, try not to be too hard on yourself. Everyone struggles with these emotions. You are not abnormal or weak for hosting negative feelings. No one should speak down to you for feeling this way.

> 26. *Write about what you are unhappy about, today. Work through these feelings.*

The written word is an amazing thing. Use it to your advantage, today. Write, write, write, and clarify the murky business of your soul. Why are you sad? How do you best fight your own sadness?

> 27. *You are not isolated. You know you can go to others and let their happiness be yours, too.*

You are empathetic. You know that you can instantly be cheered up when you witness happiness in other people's expressions. Your loved ones' happiness is particularly valuable. Seek out your loved ones in this trying time.

> 28. *You confront feelings of shame and discover their true source. You know that to overcome shame, you must recognize it.*

You should not feel ashamed. If you do, confront that feeling head on. Discover precisely why you feel the way you do, and find a solution. Demolish this feeling.

> 29. *In the end, your sadness will better you.*

You can learn from sadness. You can use your sadness to drive you to achieve something. In some way, your sadness will help you in your quest to improve.

> 30. *You are a determined individual.*

You are determined to endure the worst this world can throw at you.

Chapter 32
On Happiness

Happiness is elusive, bizarre, and even escapes description. It's one of the things that we as a society most value. We are taught to pursue what make us happy. However, we don't often know what makes us enduringly happy. Sometimes, we achieve a goal and are filled with disappointment because we expected it would make us happier than it did.

This indicates a misunderstanding of what makes us happy and what happiness really is. The truth is that happiness doesn't last. Nobody is ever completely pleased with their lives, no matter how successful they are. We will always want a new and better result than what we have achieved up until that point. That is okay. We have to teach ourselves to understand and be happy while progressing toward our goals. We will never stop progressing, and that is beautiful. If you let it, progress can be the key to your happiness.

Even Al Franken's Saturday Night Live character, Stuart Smalley, realizes the importance of overcoming your critical inner voice. In their book, I'm Good Enough, I'm Smart Enough, and Doggone It, People Like Me!: Daily Affirmations by Stuart Smalley, Franken (1992) describes the struggle with that critical inner voice and the eventual realization that you can accept and appreciate its existence without believing the things this critical inner voice espouses.

The Affirmations

1. *The world is wonderful. You are grateful for this day, no matter what it brings.*

Yes, no matter how hard our lives become, the world is still an incredible miracle. The world is a chance - a transient chance - to do something meaningful. Your life is the best thing, the only thing that you have. It would be best if you treasured every breath you take.

2. *There is beauty in everything around you, if only you give yourself the time to find it.*

From time to time, we all lose our sense of perspective. The world seems dark and cruel and filled with small-minded people. If it seems that way, know it won't seem that way forever. There are beautiful things and situations within your line of sight every day. You can choose to notice these things.

3. *Happy moments are always on their way. When one has gone, another one is coming to take its place. You simply have to actually wait a short period of time.*

Never lose faith in good times and positive feelings. Things will improve, despite the fact that it may not seem to be the case at the moment. You know they will because you are working to improve. Don't worry. The pendulum will swing back, and you will be happy again.

4. *You appreciate the little, valuable, wonderful things in your life. When you recognize one of these things, you smile. It would be best if you thanked them.*

Practice recognition and gratitude. We are imperfect and at times cynical. It can be difficult for us to see what makes our lives worth living. Put in the effort, every day, to see these things and to appreciate them.

5. *You understand that the secret to enduring happiness is gratitude and empathy.*

There is no permanent happiness. There are only moments that seem to pass too soon. That said, you can make your moments of happiness last a little longer, or a lot longer, by practicing genuine gratitude for the good things in your life. You can also be grateful for the bad. You learn and grow most in periods of adversity.

> 6. *You understand that the pursuit of happiness can make you very unhappy. Instead, you appreciate the things in your life right now that bring you joy.*

We don't know what makes us truly happy. If we hang all our hopes on the wrong thing, believing it will make us happy - and it doesn't - this can be absolutely devastating. Do not chase happiness. Do not believe that achieving your goals will make you permanently happy. Happiness is more complicated than that.

> 7. *Happiness is not only on the horizon. It surrounds you every day.*

You can find bits of happiness in your life, every day. You can notice how often you are happy, instead of letting these moments pass and convincing yourself you were never happy at all. Be self-aware enough to notice your happiness.

> 8. *You understand the positive power of a smile. You smile for yourself.*

Smiling more frequently can indeed improve your mood. Smiling is an easy, free, simple way to become a little happier. So, why aren't you smiling? Why aren't you trying to make your loved ones smile?

> 9. *You are a happy individual. You are a happy individual.*

Don't allow yourself or anybody else to convince you differently. You are happy. You see the things worth celebrating and worth being thankful for in your life. You know that sadness passes, and you work to improve yourself every day. You are, on the whole, a happy person.

> 10. *You promote happiness in others and feel happy for having done so.*

To try and make others smile or laugh is admirable. It is such a kind and considerate thing to do. You understand the importance of happiness and its fickle nature. You can make others happy. You want to because you are a kind and empathetic human being.

11. *You find happiness in the happiness of others. You share their joy.*

The joy of others is beautiful. You see it and your heart, too, will be filled with it. Let your appreciation for the happiness of others benefit you in this way.

12. *Make a list of the things and people you are grateful for in your life. You know that these things/people are wonderful aspects of your life.*

Gratitude will help you to find happiness and stay happy. While you are counting your blessings, keep in mind that you might be deprived of them at any time. It would be best if you appreciated what you have while you have it.

13. *You value hope and hard work. You recognize that you are hopeful and hard-working.*

You are able to work hard and for long periods of time because you have beautiful hope. You are inspired to keep working for yourself in the hopes that happiness is on the horizon. Indeed, happiness is on the horizon. You only have to wait for it.

14. *Your happiness is organic and precious.*

There is no use in attempting to force oneself to be joyful. It will not feel right. In fact, it may aggravate the problem. Instead, do things that have made you happy in the past and promote happiness in others. This will help to make you happier.

15. *You spend time with happy people. You appreciate their influence on your mood.*

Find joy for yourself in the joy of others. People who are happy are good influences. Especially in times of distress, surround yourself with these cheerful people to help remind you that there are things worth being happy about in the world.

16. *You know that happiness lasts longer when you recognize and give thanks for it.*

We can forget that we were ever happy if we do not properly recognize moments of happiness. When you are happy, stop for a moment and say it. Tell people you are happy. Remember, later on, that you were happy at that moment.

17. *Your happiness is important. It helps you to remain positive and productive.*

Your happiness is a tool. When you are happy, it is easy to do the things that honor your short and long-term goals. Furthermore, honoring your short and long-term goals makes you happy. It's a wonderful cycle.

18. *You are generous with your friends and loved ones. You are happy when you have made them happy.*

You know that the people in your life deserve to be happy. So, try to make them that way. You are kind and loving toward the important people in your life because they deserve it. Besides, they have and will continue to return the favor.

19. *You love your own happiness. You know that you deserve to feel happy and fulfilled in your life.*

Romanticize your happiness. Know that you are your best self when you are fully, purely happy. Happiness may be difficult to maintain now, but in practicing gratitude, you ensure that you will feel it more often and more powerfully.

> 20. *You are focused on having a positive mindset. Everything is colored by your thoughts.*

The same situation can have entirely different outcomes, depending upon the people involved. The pessimist tends to learn very little and to gain very little. On the other hand, the optimist learns and grows in spite of the circumstances.

> 21. *You are working to become happier, to appreciate happiness more.*

You deserve congratulations for your hard work. People work all their lives, they pursue happiness for as long as they can. You are participating in this age-old pursuit. However, you are changing it, too. You are managing your perception of what happiness is. In so doing, you make sure you will be happy.

> 22. *Today is another chance to notice the things and people that make you happy.*

Do not go around blind to the things that really matter. Notice and love. Let yourself notice and love in every moment of every day.

> 23. *You are worthy of happiness.*

You do not deserve to feel sad. You deserve to feel content. Let yourself be happy. Do not spend a single moment depriving yourself of that most valuable emotion. Completely reject the idea that you are unworthy.

> 24. *Yours is a success story.*

Have faith in the story that you're telling. You may not see it yet, but that's because you don't know the ending. One day, everything will make sense to you. When everything finally comes together, you'll feel complete and content with yourself. Be sure of it.

25. Your life is full of joy.

There is joy all around you, at all times of the year. You need only look for it. There are always things in your life to be happy about. Remember how precious and rare the phenomena around you are - your life, itself, should cause you to rejoice.

26. Happiness helps you to be more productive.

When you are satisfied with your work, you will do more. So, why shouldn't you be happy all the time? Accept happiness when it comes, and see how productive you can be.

27. You believe in moments of true, undiluted happiness. You notice and appreciate them when they occur.

There are such beautiful, happy moments in this world. You know they exist. You wait for them with bated breath.

28. You are good. You are happy with who you are.

You deserve to be satisfied with yourself. You are a wonderful thing.

29. You will lead a happy life.

Every moment of today, tomorrow, and the following day will be jam-packed with happy occurrences. You will manifest happiness.

Chapter 33
Setting Short-Term Goals

Short-term goals are vital to our happiness and productivity day to day. They push us to develop better habits and continue forth toward larger, more challenging goals. You will learn through the repetition of these many affirmations that short-term goals are critically important to your mental and physical well-being. You will discover over several days how good it feels to consistently achieve something. You will then reinforce this positive behavior through congratulatory affirmations.

I know that it is difficult to keep your eyes on the prize. It's even more difficult to remain focused when you are not practiced in doing so. You cannot expect yourself to meet a demanding and effort-intensive goal when you haven't taken your first "baby-steps." You aren't a sprinter right now because you haven't even crawled yet. It will take time to build the abilities that will allow you to consistently attain your broad objectives.

With these affirmations, you will set short-term goals that train your body and mind to work steadily. You will learn that you are capable of setting and meeting goals. You will build up toward the goals that are most challenging and most important to you.

The Affirmations

1. *You will set a goal this morning. You will have reached this goal by nighttime. You will be proud of yourself for this small victory.*

It doesn't have to be a large, impressive goal. Just do something you would not otherwise have done, something that benefits you in a small way. You deserve to accomplish something, however small, today. Small accomplishments add up over time.

> 2. *You can set and meet a short-term fitness goal today. You might take a walk, go for a bike ride, or do another refreshing activity. That is within your power.*

Honor your body. You need fresh air and to get your heart pumping a little faster. You'll benefit from the adrenaline rush. If you want to sharpen your mind, keep yourself in good physical shape. You'll be happier for putting in that effort.

> 3. *Today is yours to make of it what you will.*

Take charge! What do you want to do today? What do you want to achieve? You will decide to make this day an empowering one. You can prove to yourself what you are made of. You can make today an incredible day!

> 4. *Make a list of your short-term goals somewhere. You recognize the importance of putting something on paper. Your goals are real. You remind yourself of them whenever you look at that page.*

Putting your thoughts to paper can be a powerful tool. When you do it, you in some way make the words and the ideas more real than they may have been before. It can be easier to realize your goals after you have written them down.

> 5. *You value your progress toward achieving short-term goals.*

The process is as important and influential to your development as the achievement itself, if not more so. You should appreciate the moments leading up to the achievement for all they are worth, not only the end result.

6. *You celebrate appropriately once you have met one of your goals. You understand the power of positive reinforcement.*

It's all about positive reinforcement! When you have accomplished something, reward yourself appropriately. You deserve to recognize your achievements fully. Moreover, rewarding yourself for exhibiting good behavior will encourage you to behave that way in the future.

7. *You are proud of the goals that you have set for yourself. You carry them with you with pride.*

Remember what you have achieved. Too quickly and too often, we might forget the things which make us proud of ourselves. If you have to, make a list of the things you accomplish. Add to that list every day, as you work hard to meet your goals.

8. *Your goals are achievable. You work to achieve them every day.*

You can reach your goals. It's vitally important that you trust yourself to meet them, even when they seem so far out of reach. You can do it. That slogan should be repeated over and over in your head. You can. You have no room for doubt in your mind.

9. *Your goals are meaningful to you. They make you feel good.*

Working toward your goals is an honorable thing. Make sure you continue to understand how important your goals are and why. Your goals are rooted in your deepest desires. You honor them and yourself with your work.

10. *Your goals reflect well on you. You inspire others when you share your goals and progress with them.*

It feels good to share your passions and accomplishments with others. Further, it can help you to reach your goals faster and more easily when you have expressed your pride in them to others. The process can seem shorter and less arduous when you remind yourself of how much the goal means to you.

> 11. *Short-term goals help to ensure that you will reach your long-term goals. You are disciplined and self-assured.*

You know that meeting small goals first will help you to reach larger ones later. Further, these smaller goals can be a part of the larger goals you have set for yourself. Meet your smaller goals with the knowledge that they prepare you for larger ones.

> 12. *You find your progress toward your goals fulfilling. You know that working toward goals is what makes you better.*

Your progress is exciting and new. You know you can learn things about yourself throughout your progress, which can help you to refine your strategies. You can pursue success a little more swiftly every day.

> 13. *You will establish healthy and sustainable goals.*

You must make sure that the goals you are dedicating yourself to are worthy of your time and effort. If they do not make you a better person, you should abandon them as quickly as possible. Each of your goals should be worthwhile.

> 14. *Once you have met one goal, you will discover another, new goal to pursue. You recognize that continual self-improvement is possible. You know that you can always be a little better than you were before.*

You'll strive to be better until you die. That's the best sort of life. At no point should you be idle because there are always going to be parts of ourselves that could use a tad more work? Don't be scared of this reality. There's nothing nobler than changing for the better.

> 15. *You are powerful. You prove it with every day of hard work.*

It takes power to achieve all you have done. It takes power to continue to push forward and achieve more. You are an immensely powerful person. Be proud of you who are and who you will eventually become.

> *16. You are motivated to meaningful goals. Write down a few more!*

You can never have enough goals, so long as you can honor them all simultaneously. Make sure your goals do not conflict in any way.

> *17. You know that the goals you make help to determine the kind of person you are. You make meaningful and attainable short-term goals.*

You are in the process of changing this very minute. Similarly, you are in pursuit of your goals in this very minute. The goals you choose to pursue will determine the direction of your personal growth.

> *18. You evaluate the importance of your short-term goals. You understand why you are fighting to achieve each one.*

Never lose perspective. Remind yourself constantly of the importance of your goals and why your goals are meaningful. If you remind yourself, you will not lose sight of your goals.

> *19. Working toward your goals brings you joy.*

Hard effort and devotion will bring about a sense of fulfillment. Find it. Know that your work has a value that merits celebration. Joy should not be reserved for when all the work is over but should be present throughout every stage of the process.

> *20. Your short-term goals bring immeasurable value to your life.*

Short-term goals can help you in numerous ways, and you recognize that. You want to make the most of your short-term goals, so you ask what benefits you can gain in the pursuit of each. Incorporating this question into your work helps you to improve more quickly.

21. You will embrace difficult tasks today.

No matter how grueling, strenuous, or stressful, the task will seem simple today. You are ready for it. You are excited to tackle this wondrous challenge. Take on more than your share today and know that you will be all the stronger for having done so.

22. You will learn to concentrate your efforts toward achieving something important.

To focus is a hugely valuable and transferable skill. Each day, you lengthen your attention span. You work to make your focus sharper as you fight to meet your goals. As a result of a clearer focus, you are more productive and successful.

23. You are on the right track. You trust that you are on the right track.

Never doubt it: this is where you are meant to be at this place in time. You will choose where to go from here and where to go from there and so on. You are making the best choices you can. You are learning, changing, and growing happier.

24. You are committed to making real change in your life. You are committed to achieving great things.

This commitment will shine through you in all that you do and all that you achieve. People will know when they see you that you are formidable in your focus and nerve. They will know that you are a person prepped to do powerful things.

25. You know how to chase what you want.

Through trial and error, you have developed an effective way to pursue your goals. You continue to perfect your method as you work.

> 26. *You visualize your success. You know how it will feel and what it will mean. You know it is worth it to you.*

Success will mean a lot to you. You eagerly pursue it, excited by the prospect of the additional happiness it will bring. You know it will make you happy and mean that you are dynamic and strong. You know it is worth the world.

> 27. *Your short-term goals help to improve your discipline.*

Discipline will serve you well in all areas of life. You are grateful that the way you move through the world and learn affords you greater discipline.

> 28. *Your short-term goals give you additional self-confidence.*

Because you set and meet your short-term goals consistently, you are filled with confidence. You know that you can be trusted. You know that you can get the job done.

> 29. *You are grateful that you are able to work to achieve your goals.*

Some don't pursue their goals. Some can't pursue their goals. You, however, belong to neither of these groups. You are able to honor your goals through the active pursuit of them. You are able to make yourself the very best you can be.

> 30. *Your goals show you what you are made of.*

You test your mettle every day as you pursue your short-term goals. Through this process, you learn what type of man you are. You learn what type of man you are to become.

31. You are choosing to meet your goals.

You do have the choice. Whether you meet your goals or fail is entirely up to you. Choose wisely.

Chapter 34
Setting Long-Term Goals

Words and genuine beliefs are powerful, powerful things. You can manifest your success and happiness by using the right words. Studies consistently prove that self-affirmations are valuable to the body and mind. Yogananda, in his book Scientific Healing Affirmations, even goes so far as to suggest that positive affirmations can affect the physical body's ability to heal itself. He contests that repeated affirmations can activate inactive "life energy". Admittedly, that's a little out there. However, the positive effects of affirmations have been documented extensively. They may not be able to heal your physical wounds, but they can certainly, without a doubt, heal your mental and emotional ones.

The focus here is on helping you overcome obstacles to reach your long-term goals. The affirmations will help you shed your past behaviors and hang-ups to do what is right for you now. Over many days, you will learn that your goals, however impressive, are indeed within reach. You can unlock the version of yourself that will meet your goals. Every affirmation deals with the nerve and resilience required to faithfully pursue your long-term goals.

The Affirmations

1. *Every day is an opportunity to take a small step toward achieving remarkable change.*

You are working for drastic results. You understand that drastic results take time, and you don't want or need to rush it. You will figure things out in time. Make small changes that eventually accumulate into larger ones.

2. *You will be patient with yourself as you work toward your goals.*

Very few goals worth reaching come easily. It takes so much time. It takes everyone time to become the best versions of you. Understand this and embrace the slow and, at times, unsteady nature of the progress.

3. *The process toward achieving your goals is as useful to you as actually achieving them.*

It's true what they say: it's not about getting anywhere; it's about getting there. Start loving the work because that's what life is composed of. A life lived well is a constant process of self-improvement.

4. *You understand that your ambition is what makes you a better individual.*

Ambition can make you selfish, but like most qualities, it is two-sided. It can hurt you, and it can help you. Ambition sometimes gets a bad rep, but people neglect to notice that ambition drives people to improve and succeed. Your ambition is powerful.

5. *Your long-term goals are meaningful to you.*

Keep your sights set on your goals. People sometimes forget their aspirations if they fail to remind themselves of what is important. Allow yourself to not become one of those individuals. Remind yourself of your goals and why you want to pursue them. Then, do something productive that will help you meet your goal.

6. *Make a list of your long-term goals. You are aware of how effective it may be to write down your objectives and then read them back to yourself.*

Realize that the written word has a sort of magic to it. When filled with purpose and intention, it can remind you of what is most important. It can push you to work and to succeed. Let this exercise give you strength today.

7. *Your long-term goals are important to you. You trust yourself to meet these goals.*

You trust and know that one day you will meet your goal. You have dispensed with doubt because, frankly, it was never useful to you. You pursue your goals with a headstrong vitality. You know that you deserve to meet these goals.

8. *Your goals are empowering. You know that it is endlessly useful to set long-term goals and keep them in your mind.*

Your goals are tools. They keep you busy, productive, and happy. To have goals is to have reasons to live, act, and love. Recognize that your goals are an important part of your identity. Recognize that you determine your goals and how you go about achieving them.

9. *You are the driving force responsible for making progress, little by little, toward your most lofty goals.*

It is important to realize and reaffirm your total agency. You call the shots, chief. Every one of your actions, good or bad, aligned with your goals or misaligned, is yours. You decided to do that. Try to make good decisions.

10. *You are happy that you have these goals to guide you in your life.*

Goals are so vital to leading a good life. You count your goals as blessings because they are just that. Make sure you continue to set and meet small goals. Make sure you continue to set and meet larger ones, too. These are what push you to improve.

11. *Long-term goals help you to keep your life in perspective. You are a strong and dependable person.*

You know you are strong and dependable because you have to be to set and meet these long-term goals. These goals require slow, forceful, consistent work. You put the work in, and in so doing, prove yourself. You know you will meet your goals.

> 12. *You appreciate slow progress. You know that self-improvement, and life in general, is an endurance sport.*

Life is not a sprint: it's a marathon. You must maintain a speedy but consistent pace. You have to pace yourself to be as successful as possible. If you push too hard at the start, you risk having to stop and give up entirely.

> 13. *Your long-term goals are always on your mind. You are dedicated and intelligent. You will meet these goals in time.*

You remember the most important things. You know what is driving you forward in this life. Your long-term goals are always in the back of your mind, informing everything you do or say. They help you to behave in the best way.

> 14. *You feel happiest when you behave in a way aligned with your goals.*

You derive happiness from the pursuit of your long-term goals. These are the aspirations that define the very core of who you are. You are pleased to have the opportunity to work toward them. You are happy that they have entered into your mind and changed it.

> 15. *You love the potential you are filled with.*

There's something so beautiful about potential. The thought that you can do anything, be anyone, is so wonderfully freeing. Internalize that you are free to do whatever will make you happiest. You are free to become a greater self.

> 16. *You find happiness in the pursuit of your long-term goals.*

Attempting to improve yourself will ensure that you are happier because you have trained yourself to find the beauty in good things. Being productive makes you enduringly happy. You will fight to stay productive.

> 17. *You understand that the happiest people are constantly pursuing a new goal. The happiest of people improve themselves constantly.*

Your long-term goals are infused with a promise of happiness. However, so is their pursuit. You look to your friends and loved ones, and you see that the happiest and most successful are never completely still. They have goals that align with their deepest values.

> 18. *Your goals make a difference in the quality of your day.*

Having goals will make your day feel more meaningful. It will make your day happier. It will make you feel more fulfilled as you travel through the world. All that is required is that you remind yourself of your objectives.

> 19. *You share your goals with others. Your friends can help you improve upon these goals and/or build new goals altogether.*

Collaboration with trusted friends is a great way to encourage your continued improvement. The individuals in your life who are concerned about you will aid you in determining the best course of action for you. Even better than you do, they may know what sorts of goals will make you happiest.

> 20. *Your long-term goals are achievable. You make progress toward them little by little, day by day.*

Trust that your goals are possible to achieve. If you work hard enough, and if your goals are truly reflective of your innermost values, you can reach your goals. You are not scared of the time or strength it will take. You have enough time and strength in abundance.

> 21. *You are a disciplined and remarkable person.*

Do not forget that you are strong and important. You are incredible. You can do all the things you wish to do to become the person you want to become.

> 22. *Your long-term goals make you excited about your future and whatever it will bring.*

While the present is the most important time, your future is also important. Your long-term goals ensure that you are headed toward a desirable future filled with astonishing success.

> 23. *You work consistently and intelligently to reach your goals.*

Work smart. You have to be self-aware enough throughout the process to realize the quality of your work and whether something needs to change. If you need to rest, then rest. If you need to work more quickly, you do. Little adjustments should constantly be made.

> 24. *You deserve success.*

You are worthy of it. No matter what you may believe at present, you are a wonderful person deserving of every single one of your laurels. Allow yourself to celebrate. Allow yourself to be happy and to feel fulfilled. Your success is well-earned.

> 25. *Even a lack of progress, or lateral movement, will help you discover your priorities.*

Every adjustment is an opportunity to see what you are aiming for more clearly. Your values are obscured, hidden deep within you. When you modify a goal, you are doing so to honor that deep value. Keep your eyes peeled and see what it is you are truly hoping to achieve. See what you are aiming for.

26. You can do fantastic things.

You have done and you will do great things. Great things for yourself, and, better yet, great things for others. Work hard and be generous.

27. Your future is bright.

You are so lucky to have the prospects you have. You are working to improve every part of yourself and every aspect of your life! Naturally, your future is brilliantly bright, filled with the happiness you have yet to feel.

28. Your goals are worth the extra energy you expend. You are a fighter.

Do not become tired and do not become overwhelmed by stress or the amount of work you have. You can do this. You can do it, no matter how long it takes. Instead of feeling doubt or fear, feel the excitement. This work is so meaningful to you.

29. You are passionate. You put everything into your work.

You give it your all because you know it's important. You know that valiant efforts define your life.

Conclusion

Was there a change in yourself this year that you were surprised by? It's incredible that you can make monumental strides when you dedicate your mind to it. It might take everything you have to remain focused and remind yourself of your deepest desires every hour of the day, but when you do, the results are absolutely incredible. This book is about positive change. It's about how difficult it is to change and how beautiful it is when you do. It is a book that seeks to motivate black men to make changes. I hope it did that for you.

Take this time to reflect upon the person you were before you read this book. You should have improved your self-esteem, taken on better habits and goals, and gained a more mature understanding of your emotional state and physical needs. Is that right? As you look back on this year of progress, of slow and sure change, do you feel happy? Have you learned that the process is as beautiful as the finished result? Indeed, what is the most important lesson you have learned this year?

These questions are not for my sake. I cannot hear or ponder your responses at all. The final exercise of this book is to take an honest look at what you can achieve. Take the time to evaluate yourself and the rate of change you eventually settle into. Approach it like a scientist might, determining the energy expenditure needed for the tangible, positive results. I hope you found it an interesting read. Only you know that. If it was, please read on. If it not, perhaps affirmations are not for you right now. That's all right, too. You'll find something that works better this season.

Affirmations are only as powerful as your belief in them. You are still reading because you maintained a great faith in affirmations and in yourself. That is a remarkable feat of psychological strength. You should be incredibly proud of yourself for sticking through to the end. Many others gave up part way through. You persisted, and that speaks volumes about your character. It speaks volumes about your value and ability to achieve drastic, positive change. The affirmations were successful because you are a self-aware and brilliant person. I take no credit for your results: it was all you.

If these affirmations were helpful, here is what you do next: think back on the commitments that had the most significant effect on you. Make a list of them. Once you have accumulated a large list, try to determine why these affirmations were potent. Determine what in these words drove you to change in positive ways.

Once you have isolated the common denominators, develop your affirmations based on this idea. You will then have created a shortlist of affirmations tailored specifically to you. You can continue to build affirmations for yourself in this way and thus have even more purposeful and productive days. Make sure that the affirmations you create are rooted deeply in kindness. While they are concerned first and foremost with your continued productivity, they must be prevailingly kind.

In the short-term, cruel words might motivate you to push yourself harder; but in the long-term, they will destroy you and leave you empty. I don't mean to scare you; I mean to wake you up. Don't speak to yourself if what you have to say isn't coated in love and acceptance.

This book should have helped to recalibrate your mind. It should have pushed you to work on something new every month and to better yourself every day. Do not let time away from these affirmations ruin all the progress you have made. Stick true to your values and the behaviors that work for you.

This book focused a great deal on the importance of determination and consistency. Frankly, the importance of these two characteristics cannot be overstated or repeated too many times. Your decision led you through this book, through the various affirmations, improving yourself all the while. More importantly, you were consistent. You came back day after day, even though you were exhausted, and it became more difficult. You demonstrated throughout the reading process an incredible amount of strength. You astound people when you put your all into achieving your goals. I am astounded that you are still reading.

This book helped you to understand and value the most important things in your life. It encouraged you to love yourself, your goals, and the those dearest to you. Ultimately, these three aspects are most important to consider. They are the three things that you should never forget. I hope as we advance, you will honor these things with positive behaviors and the continued incorporation of affirmations into your daily life. Now, you must understand the incredible power of words to remind us of our values and inspire us to act well. It would be best if you respected these words. You must choose your words carefully and mean what you say.

Black Man, **YOU ARE** valuable to your family. The world may see you as "just another black man", but we see you as a necessity to the family structure. Why are you a necessity, you may ask? The answer is simple. It brings back balance to the family. Our young men need to see a healthy relationship between a man and a woman, just as our young girls need to see one.

We need you to teach our young men how to lead their family, our young girls how to respect themselves and the men in their lives. **TODAY IS THE DAY YOU** take control and decide how you are going to form a healthy relationship and rebuild the family unit.

www.ingramcontent.com/pod-product-compliance
Lightning Source LLC
Chambersburg PA
CBHW070458120526
44590CB00013B/687